Direct Your Own Damn Movie!

Direct Your Own Damn Movie!

Lloyd Kaufman
with Sara Antill and Kurly Tlapoyawa

Routledge
Taylor & Francis Group

LONDON AND NEW YORK

First published 2009 by Focal Press

First published 2016 by Routledge
2 Park Square, Milton Park, Abingdon, Oxfordshire OX14 4RN
605 Third Avenue, New York, NY 10017

First issued in hardback 2016

Routledge is an imprint of the Taylor and Francis Group, an informa business

Library of Congress Cataloging-in-Publication Data
Kaufman, Lloyd, 1945–
  Direct your own damn movie! / Lloyd Kaufman.
    p. cm.
  Includes bibliographical references and index.
  ISBN 978-0-240-81052-2 (pbk. : alk. paper) 1. Motion pictures—Production
and direction. 2. Kaufman, Lloyd, 1945– 3. Independent filmmakers—
United States—Biography. I. Title.
  PN1995.9.P7K382 2009
  791.4302′33—dc22

                                                                    2008046548

British Library Cataloguing-in-Publication Data
A catalogue record for this book is available from the British Library.

ISBN 13: 978-1-138-14109-4 (hbk)
ISBN 13: 978-0-240-81052-2 (pbk)

This book is lovingly dedicated to Patricia Swinney Kaufman, who has lovingly directed her own damn husband for 35 years.

Contents

Foreword (Maybe Backward)

by Mark Neveldine and Brian Taylor

We made our own damn movie, and we think it's smart of Lloyd to tell you to make your own. Seriously, who the fuck else is going to make it? It's on you, your deal, your responsibility to the independent thinkers of the world. Lloyd and his many partners (both sexual and professional) have made a career of making their own damn films.

To steal a quote from somebody who I'm sure said something like this, we ask,

"Who isn't a fan of Troma films??"

Simple . . . people who have never seen a Troma film. Watching a Troma flick is the perfect solution for a stressful world. When you go to the Troma spa, you can bathe in a soothing vat of warm puke and chunky blood. Sounds of murder will dance in your head, and the political undertones will half-bake in your cerebral cortex. We stand here today, not only as two fans of Troma Films, but as two of its unlikeliest soldiers — a directing team who makes movies for the studios (at least for now).

NEVELDINE:
It's 1996 and I'm auditioning for what will become the cult classic (yes, I abuse the term loosely, like my stool) *Tromeo & Juliet*. I was thrilled like a gay man at Fubar at my chance to work with the people who created *The Toxic Avenger, Class of Nuke 'Em High*, and *Sgt. Kabukiman, NYPD*!

After preparing my overly dramatic monologue for five minutes and fixing my hair for two hours, I stepped in front of some young filmmakers and spewed out my shitty prose. I finished, wiped my forced tears, looked up, and waited eagerly for the response. The young man at the table said, "You're really great. . . . TOO great . . . we're looking for something else." I blew it. My big shot and I were too fuckin' great. The next day I bought a video camera and started calling myself a DP (director of photography). I always like using the term "DP" because of the connotations—like Dumb Person. I thought, "I'll show these pricks how too-fuckin'-great I am!"

Cut to five years later in LA where I met my writing/directing partner, Brian Taylor, who also apparently called himself a DP (but actually was) and we created the greatest industry scam known as neveldine/taylor . . . we put my name first because I have low self-esteem. Brian says it was because it was in alphabetical order, but I'm unable to confirm this at the time of print.

FIGURE FM1 *Brian Taylor (left) and Mark Neveldine (right) visit Lloyd Kaufman (middle) as he completes his 337th hour of community service along Route 95.*

TAYLOR:

Reading Neveldine's account of his failed Troma audition, I can't help but wonder why he didn't just skip all that "acting" nonsense and start blowing choad? He was a shoe-in for the part, and knowing Lloyd, those alligator tears would've been all too real. But then again, maybe that's what Lloyd is trying to teach us in a nutshell: *suck your own damn dick.*

Lloyd Kaufman is a hero in this bizarre business of moviedom. In a system corrupted and polluted by compromise, politics, and straight up pussy-mopping cowardice, Lloyd has none of it. He's a true independent — a maverick if you will. His lineage includes all the great names of fetish-driven nutcase exploitation — Russ Meyer, John Waters, Herschell Gordon Lewis, Mel Gibson. . . He does exactly what he wants and challenges us to love and devour it. Which, of course, we do.

All of the contributing writers in this book (all more talented than us) guide you along a spiritual path to the holy land — the land where you have a completed movie that you can brag about to your high school friends. So how did we do it? Well, we came up with our own damn idea, we wrote our own damn treatment, then we wrote our own damn screenplay, then we directed and camera-operated our own damn movie.

We had the pleasure of finally meeting the brilliant Lloyd Kaufman at the 2007 TromaDance New Mexico Film Festival. One of our stunt men, Kurly Tapalapaloosa-something-or-other made the introduction and Brian and I were quick to ask Lloyd to star in our feature film, *Game*. After long negotiations and sweaty nights, Lloyd agreed and we shot his whole starring role in about two hours. Lloyd's desperate-for-an-Oscar performance for *Game* was so powerful that we immediately cast him as the soon-to-be legendary Maintenance Worker #1 in *Crank 2*. Let's just say that if these two movies are ever released, Lloyd will have to change his e-mail, and maybe his sex.

So this is the foreword or backward that we have written in honor of some of the greatest damn flicks of all time — all written or directed or produced or simply inspired by the mad genius Lloyd Kaufman. A truly compassionate man (or possibly woman) who is one of the funniest, most charming, coolest people we've ever met. Thank you for being you, Lloyd. Now go direct your own fucking movie! And if this foreword sucks, then maybe Stuart Gordon can re-animate it for us.

neveldine/taylor

Foreword Part II

by Lemmy Kilmister

So here I am writing the "short sidebar" for Lloyd "Woops-a-Daisy" Kaufman who is a fine upstanding loony, as everybody kno.' I've been in some of his movies over 10, these many years, and I have always had a great time doing them. However, I always had only a v. sketchy idea of the plot, ~~either~~ except for 'Tromeo' 'cos I cheated and read the Shakespeare version. All in all, I think Lloyd's updated scenario worked ~~better~~ better!

I will always respect Lloyd Kaufman; God knows he has not chosen an easy row to hoe (!) but his persistence struck a chord in me (as another annoying bastard who refuses to go away!)

And good luck to all who sail in him.

Love Lemmy   LONDON July 2008

Hi Lloyd, hope you're fine etc,
what I propose as the first of 3 or 4 bits I've done
which I suggest you dot about in different
places in the book.? let me know what
you think of this idea.

love and sandwiches

FIGURE FM2 *Lemmy expresses his true feelings for Lloyd Kaufman.*

Preface

Directile Disfunction

Explosive diarrhea. Perhaps not the most unglamorous phrase in the English language ("scrotal ringworm" is at least within spitting distance), but certainly not words befitting a major-league independent film director. But we're talking about *me* here, and I'd just spent a long day on the set of *Poultrygeist: Night of the Chicken Dead* (the latest Troma blockbuster) wallowing in bucket-loads of excrement spewed forth from the substantial bowels of Joe Fleishaker.[1] In fact, I had been in Buffalo for a total of three weeks now, living in a rented church alongside 80 of my hard-working cast and crew, sharing one bathroom and a total of eight beds. The shit smeared across my suit was fake, of course. I'm all for saving a buck, but trying to collect that much real poop from the *Poultrygeist* crew would've meant feeding them something besides cheese sandwiches, and that cost a hell of a lot more than whipping up a sloppy mixture of chocolaty shit-like substance made out of whatever the production assistants could steal from the nearest A&P. Still, though, I've never heard any tales of Alfred Hitchcock wading through ankle-deep crap on his way to pin a stuffed bird in Tippi Hedren's hair.

Such were my thoughts as I rode home from the *Poultrygeist* set in the Troma Team limo. The limo, of course, is a 1989 white Subaru I inherited after my mother passed away[2] and, since directing feature-length films is clearly such a lucrative line of work, it's actually the first car I've ever owned. The worn interior was thick with the aroma of real shit, which was either psychosomatic on my part or was merely the swamp ass of my driver, Kiel. Like all members

---

[1] Joe is our 500-lb action star who has appeared in Troma films since *Troma's War* in 1986. He also plays my partner, Michael Herz, on DVD introductions and at conventions. Michael's wife has never appreciated the humor there.

[2] My mother was the direct influence behind the Troma classic *Mother's Day*, directed by none than my far more talented brother Charles. Sadly, Charles has long since given up filmmaking and now owns a successful bread factory, Bread & Cie, in San Diego.

of the Troma production team, Kiel was sleeping in the commingled filth of the entire crew (sharing a room means more money on the screen!) and likely hadn't bathed or changed clothes in at least three weeks. As we zig-zagged our way through the normal collection of winos, dope fiends, and prostitutes that populate the streets of my beloved city, I began to contemplate the impending deadline for the preface to my latest book. A preface for which I've been having a hell of a time finding the right approach. The role of director weighed heavily on my mind as Kiel dropped me at my doorstep in Manhattan and sped off into the night. And by sped, I mean squealed away at the old Subaru's top speed of 38 mph.

Shuffling in the front door of my home, lovingly decorated with "I ♥ Tromaville High School" stickers, I found Pat, my lovely wife of 35 years, fixing what she likes to call dinner. As she carefully used an atomic scale to measure miniscule amounts of mayo and tomato across two pieces of Arnold's special pre-sliced plain white paper-thin bread, I breathed in the sweet smell of home.

"Don't get that stuff on the furniture," she said, looking askance at my shit-slathered duds. I looked down at my unwashed and rank clothing, feeling somewhat out of place in our living room, decorated with exotic African* art.

"You know what's a good movie?" I asked, as Pat cut into an incredibly fattening organic tomato. "*The Naked Prey*.[3] I saw it again the other night and haven't been able to stop thinking about it."

"Who's in it?" Pat asked, deftly assembling her extravagant meal.

All I could muster in response to this painfully inconsiderate question was an exasperated "Doh!"

I adore my wife. She's the apple of my eye, the banana in my nose, and the fruit in my basket, but it was just like her to want to know who played the lead, instead of worrying about the *important* things.

"You should be asking who directed the movie, not who stood there reciting lines."

---

*EDITOR'S NOTE: Lloyd spent a year in Africa, specifically Chad, in the mid 1960s. See Lloyd's other, far better, book, *All I Need to Know About Filmmaking . . .* for all the dirty things he did to acquire his collection of African art.

[3]1966, starring and directed by Cornel Wilde, who also starred in the classic film noir *The Big Combo* (1955) as well as the beloved television movie *Gargoyles* (1972). It's very likely that Mel Gibson saw *The Naked Prey* before making *Apocalypto* (2006), as the two movies share some remarkable similarities, people in loincloths aside.

My wife, like countless others, couldn't care less about who directed the film she is viewing.[4]

"Cinema is the director's event." I loudly exclaimed![5]

Pat took a bite of her sandwich, chewed thoughtfully, and swallowed. "I like to know who I'm going to be looking at for an hour-and-a-half, not who stood behind the camera and barked orders."

I felt myself trembling. Didn't she understand that the director is King, or Queen . . . or both? Without the director — without a singular, personal vision, a passion, a driving need to tell a particular story — the actors are merely window-dressing in the latest Hollywood craptacular! Creamy froth forming at the corners of my mouth, I actually began to sputter an explanation of the *auteur* theory to my brilliant and beautiful yet infuriating wife, then caught myself before I could get as far as mentioning *la nouvelle vague*.

Because, you see, in the case of *The Naked Prey*, Pat, as in most other cases, was right: who's in it was every bit as important as who directed it. The star, Cornel Wilde, *was* the director.

Come to think of it, Pat was very often right. Even when it came to things that I was supposedly the expert on, like film directing.

I stopped twitching and stared blankly at the thin tomato slice protruding from Pat's sandwich. Goddammit, now that I thought about it, several of the most consistently good film directors were also actors — Charlie Chaplin, John Ford, John Cassavetes, Clint Eastwood ... and of course, I've done my share of prancing across the silver screen in many a cinematic classic.

"Are you okay?" Pat tenderly asked.

I nodded my head in response and started to head over to the fridge. Once again, I had learned something, even when I thought I had known it all. That's when it hit me — my beloved Patty-pie had unwittingly provided me with the solution to my preface problem.

---

[4]If you, dear reader, are one of these people, maybe you shouldn't be thinking about directing a movie at all. Unfortunately, I surveyed 800,436, 987 people regarding this matter and only 6 asked "who directed?" A damn shame.

[5]Immediately find yourself a copy of *The Director's Event*, an extremely useful and insightful book by Eric Sherman, featuring interviews with five significant directors: Budd Boetticher (*The Tall T, Seven Men from Now*), Samuel Fuller (*Shock Corridor, The Big Red One*), Peter Bogdanovich (*The Last Picture Show, Paper Moon*), Arthur Penn (*Bonnie and Clyde, Little Big Man*), and Abraham Polonsky (*Force of Evil, Tell Them Willie Boy Is Here*). I believe it's currently out of print, but you can surely find it online.

Sure, I've been a motion picture director for 40 years, but in my own life — my *real* life, not the one where I have to squash heads, sever limbs, and bathe in fake shit — my astonishing wife was, quite clearly, the director. Time and time again, she had stood up to me and given it to me straight when I had my head so far up my ass that I couldn't see past my colon. It was her singular vision that was responsible for the production that was our life. Everything from the locations (our fabulous home), the cast (our lovely, talented, and indecently intelligent children), the props (every stylish item in our house), and even the postproduction (which I suppose would be our burial plots ...). The Kaufman world was a stage, and I but a player. My wife was calling the shots. And doing a ridiculously good job of it. I was about to smile and tell my lovely wife how very lovely she was, when I was struck by another thought. Just as Pat had directed me, Pat herself had been directed, in a sense, by someone named George Roy Hill. Pat had seen Hill's film *The World of Henry Orient* as a little girl, and had decided then and there to model her life after it.

And what about all the people involved in the making of that film? Who had George Roy Hill been directed by? Where did it ever end? I felt like one of the circles in the Six Degrees of Kevin Bacon game.

"Do we have any bacon?" I asked as I pushed aside a recyclable carton of soy milk.

"You don't even eat bacon," Pat said. "Why don't I put a slice of Swiss cheese on the sandwich you'll be eating when you get out of the shower ... "

Once again, the director is directed. I guess the *auteur* theory, which I will describe in minute and excruciating detail in the coming pages, isn't black and white. Even those with control issues, like me, can, in turn, be dominated themselves. And a fresh-faced kid like you? I have plenty of experience dominating ... er ... directing young people like you. Just remember that there are no exact answers in filmmaking. Some people, like the authors of other books, will tell you that there are. But there aren't. I don't think.

The ideas and wild right-wing conspiracy theories in this book will help you to direct a movie.

It won't necessarily be a good movie.
It won't necessarily be a hit movie.

It very likely won't win any Oscars.

But it will be yours.

So just think of this book as explosive diarrhea in print. Lap it up, spit out the chunks, and excuse the smell. Hopefully you'll get something out of it, and you'll be able to direct your own goddamn fucking movie. And when your movie is finished, maybe you'll get to experience the joy of looking back and wondering why the hell you made the thing. But at least you'll have done it. And I'll have made a couple of bucks. And by then, I also may have taken a shower and gotten rid of this shitty smell.[6]

xoxo

Lloyd Kaufman

aka "Unca Lloydie"

2008

---

[6]Neither making a couple of bucks nor taking a shower are guaranteed. Please don't hold me to the shower thing if you ever meet me.

Acknowledgments

Michael Herz and Maris Herz, who have given my own damn life some direction over the last 35 years.

Jerome Rudes, who directed me toward writing my own damn book.

Elinor Actipis, William Akers, Allison Anders, Sara Antill, John G. Avildsen, Jack Beranek, Travis Campbell, Benjamin Cord, Annie Cron, Michele Cronin, Andy Deemer, Lisa Eastman, Josh Edelman, Jenna Fischer, Jonathan Foster, Stuart Gordon, James Gunn, Footnote Guy, Jeremy Howell, Evan Husney, Ron Jeremy, Charles Kaufman, Charlotte Kaufman, Lily Hayes Kaufman, Lisbeth Kaufman, Sigrun Kaufman, Susan Kaufman, Lemmy Kilmister, Roger Kirby, Avril Lavigne, Stan Lee, Lindsey Lemke, Bill Lustig, Sean McCoy, Neil McCurry, Maria de Medeiros, Mark Neveldine, Jean Prewitt, Amanda Roberts, Debbie Rochon, Eli Roth, Kenny Ryback, Penelope Spheeris, Dee Snider, Whit Stillman, Brian Taylor, Kurly Tlapoyawa, Jonathan Wolf.

And I'd like to direct a special thanks to the "Exit 47" sign on Route 95, which has provided me with some valuable and practical direction throughout the years.

Chapter one

Joining the Army of One

Rule #1 of film directing:
It is okay to drown newborn kittens, so long as they have not yet opened their eyes.

"Alright everybody," I yell into my small, battery-operated bullhorn. "Let's get into first position!"*

It is the summer of 1982. My trusty crew and I are filming a particularly steamy scene for *The First Turn-On!*, a film notable for featuring both Vincent D'Onofrio and Penthouse Pet Sheila Kennedy in their first on-screen roles.[1] The scene is a tantalizing sex romp between two attractive young actor-persons who are rolling around in the hay of a goat shit-filled barn. Lacking adequate electricity to

---

* A NOTE FROM YOUR FRIENDLY FOOTNOTE GUY: Hi Friends! I just wanted to formally introduce myself here. I will be typesetting all of the informative footnotes you see in this book. Footnoting is a very underappreciated vocation, and I really look forward to working with Lloyd and all of you awesome readers. Thanks!!

[1] Also noteworthy for Michael Herz's and my turning down Madonna, who desperately wanted a role. Which brings us to Rule #2 — don't turn down future superstars who want roles in your film. And if you do, for the love of God, at least save the audition footage to sell later.

power our light kit, we are relying entirely on two bounce cards,[2] which we have carefully duct taped to a pair of rusted pitchforks.

"Quiet for sound," I call out, meticulously framing the shot as silence falls over the barn. Before I can call "action," I am interrupted by the sound of something violently thrashing in water, accompanied by the cries of a pig being raped. This is a Troma set, so I am not surprised. But I am pissed.

"I said 'quiet' you assholes!" I shout. Part of me actually expects compliance. The noise gets even louder.

"Son of a bitch! This is why no one takes us seriously!"

Reciting a litany of curse words that would make John McCain blush, I throw my headphones off and stalk toward the barn doors, carefully avoiding the mounds of goat shit as I stomp outside. As the doors swing open, I am temporarily blinded by the sunlight. When my eyes adjust, I am confronted by the most gruesome sight I have ever witnessed:

> The owner of the farm.
> Standing over a large barrel filled with water.
> Drowning a struggling kitten.

Off to the side of the barrel, a large pile of his previous victims lay like a soggy lump of wet wigs. It's like Auschwitz, but with cats. I freeze as my brain struggles to comprehend what is going on. The farmer drops the kitten in his hand onto the pile and turns to me.

"It's alright, Lloyd. Their eyes were still closed."

He smiles widely, and there is an awkward moment where I try to determine whether to laugh or drop to a fetal position and start screaming for my mother.

This is what I learned that day . . . Apparently, if you are in a situation where you suddenly have a litter of kittens that you do not want, you are allowed to drown them if their eyes have not opened. If their eyes have, in fact, opened, then it is *not* morally acceptable to drown them. This piece of wisdom brings us to our next rule.

> Rule #3 of film directing:
> There are too many idiotic rules in filmmaking.

---

[2] I'd love to define bounce cards here, but we haven't used them since the 1980s, and frankly, the 1980s are a little fuzzy for me. I'm pretty sure they are shiny white surfaces that reflect light back at the source.

If Alejandro Jodorowsky had displayed such Pavlovian obedience to the kitten drowning rules of Hollywood, masterpieces such as *El Topo* and *Holy Mountain* would have never been made. Jodorowsky recently declared that he would rather distribute his movies for free on the Internet than have his work interfered with by major studios. He believes such an act could spark a cinematic revolution. Do these sound like the words of a man who gives a shit about following stupid rules?*

WHY YOU SHOULD (A) NOT DROWN KITTENS AND (B) BUY THIS BOOK

You may be scratching your head right about now and thinking,

"Hey Lloyd, there are millions of books about filmmaking. Why should I buy yours when I could spend that $25 on half a gallon of gas?"

To this I would answer,

"Get a bicycle."

This book that you hold in your hands contains 92%[3] of all the first-hand, real-world, road-rules knowledge that I have accumulated in my over 40 years as a director of feature length films. And what all that experience has taught me is this:

> Rule #4,008 of film directing:
> A slavish devotion to following rules as though they were set in stone only serves to stifle the creative process.

I feel that the best rule to follow is to not blindly[4] follow any goddamn rules at all.

ME ACTUALLY FOLLOWING MY OWN ADVICE

The Toxic Avenger would never have existed had it not been for Michael Herz and my decision to break convention and combine

---

* A NOTE FROM YOUR FRIENDLY FOOTNOTE GUY: It's me again! There isn't actually supposed to be a footnote here, but I just wanted to say that Lloyd is one of my favorite authors, mostly because he uses more footnotes than anyone in the universe! You know, there isn't a whole lot of work out there for a footnote typesetter, and I just wanted to say thanks, Lloyd. Footnote #4 in the book's foreword was just incredible! I ♥ Lloyd Kaufman!!

[3] I'm saving the other 8% for my next book.

[4] Especially if you are a newborn kitten who hasn't opened its eyes yet.

the genres of slapstick and gore into one film. Thanks to our willingness to break the rules, a cult film sensation was born. Not only has Toxie paved the way for my numerous free, booze-and-drug-filled, hooker-offered-but-refused, trips around the world, but directors such as James Gunn and Peter Jackson credit the film with paving the way for them to unleash their comic-horror genius upon the world.

FIGURE 1.1 *Lloyd Kaufman and Baryshnikov share a private moment at the Tanglewood Dance Festival.*

NOW IT'S YOUR TURN TO FOLLOW MY ADVICE

Now far be it for me to speak in generalities, but possibly every meaningful director[5] to ever shoot a frame of film has been a rule breaker, and the world is a far better place because of it. Who can imagine a cinematic landscape devoid of rule breakers and shit disturbers like Charlie Chaplin, Howard Hawkes, and Sam Fuller?

---

[5] The above note on *The Toxic Avenger* is not meant to imply that I include myself among other meaningful directors. I do, of course, but here I was just trying to show you how I can afford to travel around the world, usually on someone else's dime. I actually prefer dimes to airplanes, especially when it comes to the footrests.

What sets these geniuses apart is their emotional and spiritual investment in the films they were making. They managed to make each film a true reflection of themselves.[6] In this way, there is no reason why you cannot achieve the same thing. Staying true to yourself when making your film may not win you any Oscars, but it will make you a happier person.[7] And after you throw off these mortal coils, some French critic may suddenly discover that you were an underappreciated artist — a true genius. So there really is hope!

PENELOPE SPHEERIS ROCKS OUT ON ROCKIN' THE BOAT

Penelope Spheeris directed films such as Wayne's World *and the punk-rock documentary* The Decline of Western Civilization. *As a result of that film and its sequel, she is often worshipped as a goddess in the punk-rock world, and has several temples dedicated to her throughout the Midwest.*

I think a good mantra for being a filmmaker is "do what you believe in and it'll work." If you do your work for money you're really making a big mistake. I know whenever I ventured out and did something for money it really wasn't the right thing to do.

Protecting creativity is tricky, especially in the studio system. When it comes to politics, you really need to know how to ride the wave, especially if you're a woman or a minority. You have to get what you want creatively, but not piss anybody off. Unfortunately, it's a small community and a lot of people talk to each other, and if you get a bad rap, you're going to be out.

Around the time I was doing *Wayne's World,* my agent said to me, "I see that there is some dissension going on about the way certain things are being done and about getting the movie finished." He said flat out — never rock the boat until you're pay or play — until your contract is signed, don't say anything that's going to get anyone mad. Until you've got your foot in the door and people are readily paying you for your work, then you can go ahead and do things creatively in your own fashion. You've got to carefully navigate the political landscape. No one likes a bully or a prima donna.

[6] Just like Olympic ambulance chaser John Edwards did when he and his ugly mistress created films of himself to put on the Internet during his run for president of the U.S.

[7] Just look at me! It doesn't get any better than this sad old Jew.

BILL LUSTIG ON PORN VERSUS FILM SCHOOL

Bill Lustig directed such horror classics as Maniac *and the* Maniac Cop *series. He also directed a handful of hardcore porn films under the name Billy Bagg. He is no relation, however, to Lloyd's alter ego, Douche Bagg.*

FIGURE 1.2 Presidential candidate John Edwards visits Tromaville and shows off his $800 haircut.

I learned film as a passion. I read in libraries and went to New York when I was 14 or 15 and knocked on doors and applied to be a production assistant, which led to a lot of great experiences, things like *Crazy Joe* with Peter Boyle. That led to an apprentice job in a post production facility in New York, which gave me a great insight into what the film industry is like and what the final product ends up being.

A big advantage I had in the 1970s was that porno was huge. After *Deep Throat*, porn was the gold rush. At that time they were 35 mm and there was an open door policy and I was able to get jobs at 17. I learned how to position a mic and how to operate different machines — lots of things that I would never learn in film school. Storytelling is great but the craft will get you to the finish line. Today, I would advise against starting off in porn because it is incredibly different. In the 1970s, they were made with the thought of being a real film. Film stock created a discipline because with video, you can shoot as much as you want. I think that porn is a ridiculous thing. Music videos would be a good introduction. I think it's much tougher today.

I'm not a big advocate of film school. One of the things that film school underprepares people for is set etiquette. You set a chain of command to function and actually get your work done. I'm a firm believer of people being quiet on set and of a chain of command to get a film done. Exhaustion is inevitable. I have a thing I do when I am really tired — I say to myself one night at 11:30 p.m. I will tune into HBO and I'll be comfortable. That moment will be the payoff.

When it comes to directing, there is a way of having an open door for ideas without having a free-for-all. The director can either be a kind general or a prick, but still the general. Always be prepared. When a decision is made, you have to implement the decision. In the independent world, everyone has their foot in film school and that can undermine the film. No one is as confident as they pretend to be.

SUMMONING YOUR INNER DOMINATRIX

As director, the level of control you have over the production of your film is entirely up to you. Personally, I like to be as involved as possible. I have final approval on everything, from wardrobe to special effects, and props to catering. I even decide where to put the porta-potties.[8] The idea that the director is ultimately the final author and owner of her film has its roots in the *auteur* theory of the French new wave. Feel free to read the following paragraphs aloud in a pretentious French accent, or while wearing a French maid uniform, or a French tickler. I am wearing both as I write this chapter!

---

[8] *Direct Your Own Damn Movie* Hint: A good director places the porta-potties outdoors and away from the catering table.

SOMETHING GREAT THE FRENCH GAVE US, BESIDES A FANTASTIC WAY TO MAKE OUT AND A TASTY WAY TO PREPARE POTATOES

From the dawn of motion pictures up until the 1950s, every film made was essentially a studio picture. Under the fist of the studio system, it was the producer, not the director, who drove the vision of the film. The producer was responsible for shepherding the entire project from start to finish, and in the process, branded it with his own identity. Witness the recent release of the Val Lewton box set as a perfect example of this practice — every film in the set is considered a "Val Lewton film," although he didn't direct a single one. Under this system, directors were usually hired guns who worked for the studio, helping to bring the producer's vision to the screen. Can you name the guy who directed Casablanca?[9] Didn't think so.

FIGURE 1.3 *Lloyd Kaufman, imitating Lloyd Kaufman on the cover of the* Make Your Own Damn Movie *Box Set.*

This isn't to say that there weren't incredibly powerful and self-defined directors back then. There have always existed directors

---

[9] That would be Michael Curtiz. Don't ever forget that name. It'll be a Jeopardy question some day.*

  *A NOTE FROM YOUR FRIENDLY FOOTNOTE GUY: I'll remember, Lloyd. I've been preparing for Jeopardy my whole life. It's one of the benefits of typing tedious, yet informative, footnotes all day long. My head is just filled with Jeopardy worthy little-known facts!

such as D.W. Griffith and Erich von Stroheim who gave in to no man, firmly worshipping at the shrine of individual vision. Sadly, these directors were exceptions to the rule, and for many years, the producer called the shots, under the reign of supreme rulers like Irving Thalberg and Louis B. Mayer.

This style of filmmaking was challenged in the 1950s by French film critics, notably Andre Bazin, cofounder of the highly influential film magazine, *Cahiers du Cinema*. Inspired by the self-styled directors of their day, these connoisseurs of fine film advocated the idea that it should be the director, not the producer, who should be the driving force behind a film — the *auteur*[10] of the project.

I feel that our snail-sucking French brethren had it right. Every film that Troma has ever made has used the auteur theory as a guiding principle. As the author controls the book,[11] it is the director who controls the movie. This is an idea I stubbornly adhere to up to this day. You know what they say: You can take the boy out of the auteur, but you can't take the auteur out of the boy.[12]

After all, what is the point of directing a movie if you aren't going to make it your own damn movie? You didn't sign up to direct traffic on someone else's street. As the director of an independent film, you'll end up being the one left holding the bag of flaming shit when it's all said and done. It might as well be your own shit in that bag.

Lest I get carried away in my own pretentiousness, let's remember that I make movies about chicken Indian zombies,[13] monstrously deformed janitors and lusty, hard-bodied lesbians. But we all have to draw from our own life experiences. Now seems like a good time to mention another rule:

Rule #62 of film directing:
Try not to be a pretentious prick, especially when directing an independent film or writing a book on directing independent films.

---

[10]That's "author" with a French accent.

[11]I hope my editor reads this — she was quite adamant about calling this book, *Eli Roth's Slambang Super Awesome Rules of Film Directing, written by Lloyd Kaufman.*

[12]Especially if said *auteur* is not properly lubed.

[13]Troma's latest release, *Poultrygeist: Night of the Chicken Dead*, available now from http://www.troma.com. BUY TROMA!!

FIGURE 1.4 *Original poster for Spielberg's magnum opus,* Schindler's List.

ALL PRICKS, BIG AND SMALL

Speaking of pretentious assholes, let me give you an example of what type of director NOT to be. Roger Donaldson, the director of the $200 million cinematic abortion known as *Dante's Peak*, signed off on that movie as "A Roger Donaldson Film." You may not be aware of this, but having the phrase "A So-and-So Film" on your movie is a pretty big fucking deal. It implies that the director guided every step of production, that she poured blood, sweat, and tears into the movie, and that, ultimately, the film is a true representation of her artistic vision. "A (insert your name here) Film" is the cinematic signature of a true auteur. Now, are we to believe that the $200 million *Dante's Peak*, a volcano movie with no lava, was the culmination of this man's hard fought artistic vision? I saw more violent eruptions of hot, steamy liquids in *Dante's Freak*, the highly entertaining and vastly superior porn version.

Also worthy of a mention — *Dante's Peak* was released around the same time as *Tromeo & Juliet*, a movie with a $350,000 budget. While the popularity of *Tromeo & Juliet* has risen over the years, you would be hard pressed to find anyone today who gives two fucks about *Dante's Peak*, despite a marketing budget of at least $50 million compared to *Tromeo & Juliet*'s marketing budget of 79 cents.

Even though I remain one of the few true American film auteurs, a fact recognized by Japanese sensation Takashi Miike — director of such brilliant films as *Ichi the Killer* and *Audition* — I refuse to have any of my films labeled as "A Film By . . ."[14] or "A Lloyd Kaufman Film." Although I do maintain strict control over each film, filmmaking is far too collaborative an undertaking for me to claim full responsibility for the end result. And besides, I hardly consider myself worthy to stand alongside such giants as Sergei Eisenstein and Orson Wells.[15]

What type of director will you choose to be? Do you see yourself directly involved in every aspect of your film? Would you rather play it fast and loose, letting other people call the shots regarding matters not directly involved with your responsibilities. You could just crank out some hemorrhoid on celluloid like *Dante's Peak* and sign off on it as "A Film By," like Roger Donaldson, giving you the false appearance of being an auteur. Remember one thing though — putting earmuffs on a cantaloupe won't make it talk. No amount of

---

[14] John Ford did not sign *The Searchers* or any of his films as an auteur, so why should I?

[15] They are both probably a full foot taller than I am anyway, so standing alongside them would look a little ridiculous.

make believe or kabillion dollar ad campaign can suddenly make a bad film watchable.

Poultrygeist Hatching in New York City, May 9th, 2008

"A VERITABLE CLUCKWORK ORANGE..." -VARIETY

"THE BEST FILM TROMA'S EVER PRODUCED, AND CERTAINLY LLOYD KAUFMAN'S MOST ACCOMPLISHED." -C.H.U.D.

A LLOYD KAUFMAN/MICHAEL HERZ PRODUCTION

POULTRYGEIST

NIGHT OF THE CHICKEN DEAD

OPENS MAY 9TH AT THE CITY CINEMAS VILLAGE EAST 181 2ND AVE. NEW YORK, NY 10003. PH: 212.529.6998. ACCLAIMED DIRECTOR LLOYD KAUFMAN AND CAST APPEARING IN PERSON MAY 9TH!

FIGURE 1.5 *Rare photo of President John McCain in a North Vietnamese prison, c. 1966.*

MY BIG FAT BUDGET STUDIO DREAM WEDDING

"Just sign right here, Mr. Kaufman, and we can begin production immediately," bellows the fish-mouthed studio exec as he slides a thick and finely printed contract across the table. His words are punctuated by chocolately smacks of his fish lips as he gobbles down a handful of peanut M&Ms. A muffled fart noise disturbs the otherwise quiet room.

"I think you'll find everything in order."

I hold the contract in my hands as I scan over the legalese. A chance conversation about *The Toxic Avenger* at a Hollywood party a year ago led to a series of cross-country phone calls, all leading up to this moment. The moment when I sign my baby away.

I slowly take a sip of the iced tea Mr. Fish Mouth's assistant had brought to me earlier. I reach into my pocket for a pen, wondering why my assistant never brings me iced tea. My fingers fumble amongst the lint for a moment, when I feel a small prick.

"What the shit . . ." I grumble as I pull my hand out of the pocket. Sticking out of my pointer finger is a *Toxic Avenger* promotional lapel pin. Fitting, I think to myself — a pain in the ass, or the finger, right until the very end.

And why shouldn't I cash in? It's not like I'm getting any younger, and I've more than paid my share of dues.

As I look at the lapel pin, however, with the deformed, heroic visage of Toxie staring back at me, I feel a sudden rush of self-righteous indignation. There was no way in hell I was going to sign away my most precious creation to a devil-worshipping media conglomerate. No way! Until, of course, I see the part of the contract the reads "monetary compensation." I've never seen so many zeros following a number in my life. From there my eyes stumble across phrases such as "complete creative control will remain solely with Lloyd Kaufman," and "Lloyd Kaufman shall retain approval of final cut."

This contract is beautiful.

I would have to be half a retard* not to sign this thing. I click my pen into action.

"Lloyd," a voice calls out from above.

"Not now, damn it. Can't you see I'm busy?"

"Lloyd, wake up. I brought you some iced tea."

---

*EDITOR'S NOTE: I'm sure Lloyd is using the word "retard" in the kindest, most non-offensive, non-libel way that a person could possibly use that word. Maybe we could find another word, Lloyd?

Shit. I open my eyes and before me is not a contract guaranteeing my financial future and that of my great-grandchildren, but the face of my tired assistant, Sara.[16] It's 8 a.m. at the new Troma offices in Long Island City. My desk is covered in drool. I cover the spit pool with an autographed promotional still and stand up to stretch. Sara glances at my crotch, throws the plastic cup of iced tea in the direction of my desk, turns a quick 180 degrees, and retreats from my office. I look down and discover that I am sporting a serious morning boner. Also, I'm not wearing any clothes. I begin to wonder if there are any dead hookers in the building . . .

WHAT IT ALL MEANS

Maybe none of this happened. Maybe it did. I really don't remember. But what I'm trying to get across is that if you have any hope of retaining the slightest creative control over your film, not to mention your dignity, within the confines of the Hollywood system, YOU ARE DREAMING. Rid yourself now of such nonsensical fantasies. The cold, hard fact of the matter is, if you want to maintain complete control over a film project, you need to make the damn thing yourself.

Sure, there are a few noteworthy exceptions to my anti-establishment sentiment. Filmmakers such as Quentin Tarantino, Eli Roth, Penelope Spheeris, Trey Parker, James Gunn, and Todd Haynes have managed to create brilliant movies that have something to say while working within the mainstream studios. Kudos to these ingenious visionaries for accomplishing this Herculean task while retaining their edge. But they are the exceptions.

ELI ROTH SAYS . . . (FILM SCHOOL VERSUS SET EXPERIENCE)

Eli Roth grew up watching Troma films and showed the Troma classic Charles Kaufman's Mother's Day at his bar mitzvah when no girls showed up. He's kind of twisted in the head. Oh yeah, he is also the writer/director

---

[16]Turns out my former assistant, Kiel, whom I mentioned in the preface, sped off into the night in my 1989 Subaru and never actually came back, leaving me without a car or an assistant.

of Cabin Fever *and the landmark horror hit* Hostel. *See? He's twisted. Eli also appeared in Troma's* Terror Firmer *and* Tales From the Crapper, *a decision that he must surely regret.*

FIGURE 1.6

I went to film school, I loved film school. But you don't NEED to go to film school. I'm actually one of the few people from my class in film school who's directing movies, and it's not because of talent, it's really much more because of perseverance and drive, and because I was one of the few people who was willing to get coffee for people. If you wanted to be a surgeon, you wouldn't just go out and buy a bunch of tools and show up at the hospital and say "Hey! I'm ready to do surgery!" And if you wanted to be a professional basketball player, you wouldn't say, "You know what? I know everything about basketball. I watch basketball every week, I played in high school, I played in college . . . I'm going to go join the Lakers." But a lot of people think, "I know everything about movies, therefore I'm just going to be a director." The best thing you can do is get as much set experience as possible before you make your own film. Even Quentin Tarantino was a production assistant. Before *Reservoir Dogs* Tarantino made a film called *My Best Friend's Birthday*, where he spent an entire year shooting a movie on weekends — a film he never finished — and he said that's where he made all of his mistakes. Don't think that when he showed up on the first day of shooting *Reservoir Dogs* he had never been on a set before, because he had.

I would recommend being a PA on as many movies as possible. When you do that, you learn the pace of the set. You understand how long it takes to light a shot, and you watch other people make mistakes. A lot of people will take PAs for free, I was a PA for free for three or four years, or four or five years. I worked in the casting department, I worked in the editing department, I worked on set, and I really got an idea of what happens. I was the guy going "Excuse me, could you please step across the street." When you do that for sixteen hours a day, you learn the pace of it. You gain patience.

If you are SERIOUS about being a director — if you're serious — you have to move to a city that shoots movies, and you have to work on those movies. That's the best advice I can give. A lot of people feel like they're artists, they're above it, they're exempt . . . well, guess what? There are 699 other students from my class in film school who are not making movies because they felt the same way. It was me and maybe two other guys that were the ones who were willing to get coffee and here we are.

Find *The Hollywood Reporter*, look at what sets are looking for work, work on every production in every city, every state. There you have it. You can get *The Hollywood Reporter* online. You can order it. And every movie that's shooting will list their offices. You call them, stop by, drop off your resume, and tell them that you'd like to be a production assistant. Or you can work as an intern. If you're serious about it, tell them "let me intern for just a month," or "let me intern for just a week." And once they get to know you and like you and trust you, you say, "can I stay on for the whole shoot?" It's about persistence. And if you get rejected, try again, because that's what it's going to take. It's an endurance test to see just how serious you are about being a director. And if you can't handle it, quit.

HOLLYWOOD, HOT CELEBS AND HERPES

If your main desire is to be famous and live in a plush estate with your ex-model wife and your wicked coke habit, then by all means, move to Hollywood and start playing the game. Maybe it will work for you. But more likely, you will end up making films in a system that actively works to alter your vision — a system run entirely by twenty-something know-it-alls who have never heard of Fred Zinnemann[17] or seen a Charlie Chaplin movie. And that's if you're lucky. It's more likely you'll end up working at Pink's Hot Dogs and telling strangers how you'd like to make a movie someday.

---

[17] In a famous story, Fred Zinnemann, the Academy Award winning director of *High Noon*, sat down to meet with a young studio executive. The young exec asked Zinnemann what he had done in his career. Zinnemann replied, "You first . . ."*

*EDITOR'S NOTE: Lloyd, why is this story buried in a footnote?

LLOYD'S RESPONSE: It's not about me.

FOOTNOTE GUY SAYS . . . Fuck you, Editor. Great story Lloyd! Totally footnote worthy!

I, on the other hand, would rather not have my cinematic vision corrupted by some giant Hollywood conglomerate. Because of this, I remain firmly entrenched on the other side of the country. Other independent directors such as Scott Phillips of New Mexico, Chris Seaver of Syracuse, NY, and Todd Solondz of New York, NY have resisted the siren call of Hollywood and have managed to create brilliant films on their own with no budget to speak of.

The fact is, you'll probably haul in more cash by hustling hand jobs in the piss-stained alley behind the Walgreens than by directing your own film. This is certainly not a swipe at the hardworking hand job hustlers behind the Walgreens on W. 68th St., but if money is what drives you, you might want to choose another career. The battlefield is littered with the corpses of filmmakers who didn't make it, and I would hate to think of you as one of them. By the way, what are you wearing? Tell me real slow . . . real slow . . . oh yeah . . .

Have I ever told you that I love you?

But if you are an artist and the desire to create cinematic glory is bursting from within you, then let's get started.

Let's make some art!

A NOTE FROM MY EDITRIX

---------------------------Original Message---------------------------

From: elinor@repress.com
Sent: Apr 9, 2008 8:16 PM
To: Lloyd Kaufman <lloyd@troma.com >
Subject: Chapter 1

Dear Lloyd,

This chapter is pretty good-entertaining while still somewhat informative. Now that you have pulled people in a bit, I think you can begin to focus a little stronger on the actual directing tips. Can't wait to see more from you (soon)!!

We're all really excited here to see what you'll come up with!

Best,
Elinor

Sent via BlackBerry by AT&T

---------------------------End Message---------------------------

Chapter two

It's the Shit! . . . Er, Script!

A writer should have this little voice inside of you saying, tell the truth.
Reveal a few secrets here.

—Quentin Tarantino

Writing scripts sucks.

—Lloyd Kaufman

MY OWN PERSONAL PIECE OF HELL

The sun has finally set in Sin City, Nevada. The neon lights have sparked to life, bathing the streets in a kaleidoscope of color, which seem to act as homing beacons for the truly original and unique individuals who have gathered in this amazing city to participate in all forms of hedonism and decadence. They have come from all walks of life: from the model businessmen and homely housewives to the downtrodden junkies and prostitutes. The streets of Las Vegas teem with a raw energy unlike any other city on earth. Obviously, I have found myself smack dab in the middle of it all. More specifically, I'm standing near the rear of The Bunkhouse, an awesome center of counterculture activities, enjoying myself as various bands take the stage for Tromapalooza — a fund raising event, created by Christy Larson, to raise money for the TromaDance[1] Film Festival in Park City, Utah.

The people are friendly and full of energy. The music is excellent. Super Tromette Pirate and a Tromette army are here in full force. In short, I'm having a blast. Obviously, since this is MY life we're talking about here, something has to fuck it all up. It's the same thing every time, really. I'm busy signing DVDs for Troma fans, waiting for the bloody[2] T-shirt contest to begin, when one sloppy drunk after another approaches me to pitch his/her ideas for films. Not completed films that they are seeking distribution for, mind you. But IDEAS for films they think I should make. Welcome to my personal hell.*

I don't mean to sound like a bitter old Jew, but trying to fake a polite smile while listening to the same pitch from the same drunken hesher four times in a row will start to stick in anyone's ass. Don't get me wrong, I think it's fantastic when anyone has an original idea for a film. But sometimes I get the feeling that these guys honestly think that after they pitch me their idea, I stick it into a magical black box and a completed film miraculously appears out of the other side. They need to do more than repeat that idea to everyone within earshot — they need to sit down and actually put words to paper and bring that idea to life. Hell, some of the ideas that are pitched to me are actually quite good. But when I say to these guys "that's a great idea, what are you going to do with it?" They stare back at me as though I had just let out a monstrous trumpet-blast of a fart. I'm not trying to piss in anyone's punch bowl, but the fact is, a great idea alone does not a movie make. You

---

[1]TromaDance is the only truly independent film festival in Park City. We don't charge a submission fee for filmmakers, nor do we charge admission to any of the screenings. Visit www.tromadance.com and give us some money. Please . . .

[2]Not "bloody" the way that British people use the word, but actual blood-soaked shirts. There is nothing sexier, in my opinion.

*FOOTNOTE GUY SAYS: Want to hear about my personal hell? How about your entire existence being relegated to the bottom of a page. How about no one even knowing your name. Welcome to my life . . .

need to put that idea on paper and create a story that has a beginning, middle, and an end.

As I was saying . . . The problem is, writing a screenplay takes serious effort. Not everyone has the time or patience to make it happen. But if you are even remotely serious about being a filmmaker, it's something you have to learn to get done. Believe me, I know what a gigantic pain in the ass it is to write a script for a feature-length film. For example, here is an average day of writing for me:

I'm slumped in the chair behind my desk; a half-empty bottle of Popov Vodka sits next to a small glass to my right. In front of me lays a yellow notepad. I stare at it. It stares back; taunting me with its crisp, empty pages. The ballpoint pen in my hand remains unmoved and unmotivated. Finally, after seven hours of brain-wracking work, I look down at what I've written so far:

FADE IN:
INT. ABU GHRAIB PRISON-DAY.

Disheartened by my lack of progress, I inevitably rise from my chair, plop down my pen, grab my drink, and go see what's on TV. In short, I really don't like to write. In fact, I find myself getting up every ten minutes finding every excuse not to work. If this sounds like you,* this chapter may just help you find a solution to your dilemma.

---

*A NOTE FROM YOUR FRIENDLY FOOTNOTE GUY: I might have to agree with your assistant on this one, Lloyd. This doesn't sound like anyone. Who writes a screenplay on a yellow legal pad?

WHIT STILLMAN AND OSCAR

Whit Stillman sold his apartment to finance his first film, Metropolitan, *for which he received an Academy Award nomination for best original screenplay. This just goes to show that homeless people can make good movies, too.*

FIGURE 2.1 Oscar-nominated director Whit Stillman (far right) on the set of *The Last Days of Disco.*

When starting out, I think it's good to just focus on doing your own work and not worry too much about the industry. With my first film, *Metropolitan*, which in a sense is my best, the one thing I knew was that no one would be interested in it in a business sense. It had to be through friendship or enthusiasm or some sort of contact. It had to be non-business for people to get involved. I was making films underneath the union radar when I started out. There was no money and I was producing-writing-directing myself. *Metropolitan* took the long path to everything. We'd been rejected everywhere. We'd been rejected at Sundance, and no distributor wanted us. They said we weren't "commercial." And then by going to some festivals, we got into Sundance sort of through the backdoor. The film did well there but distributors didn't buy it. After Sundance, we went to the New Directors Series in New York at the Museum of Modern Art, and it wasn't until the press screening there that critics started liking us, and we finally got an offer for distribution. When the film came out, it played a really long time — I think it played in New York a total of seven months. So a lot of the academy members must have seen it in New York during its long run. So we just sent a letter, asking people to vote for it. It was the lowest expense, lowest tech campaign possible, and it got a nomination for Original

Screenplay. That was kind of great for a small film like that. Getting nominated definitely helped attract attention for its run and it helped it get some recognition when it was distributed abroad.

The thing is, like with *Metropolitan*, sometimes when you're doing something low-budget, and it's hand-to-mouth and you don't know where all the money is going to come from and you don't know what's going to happen with it, in a way it's the worst of times because there's so much uncertainty. But in a way, it's the best of times because no one cares. No one is pressuring you. They couldn't care less. And it is actually good, creatively, to work in that atmosphere. Once you're in the industry, even when people are being great to you and giving you freedom, like the great situation that we had with our two films with Castle Rock — just because you're in the industry, there are these pressures. Maybe you kind of rush the editing. "Oh, can you make it shorter? Can you make it tighter?" Even though the decisions were ours, sometimes it's better when no one cares about what you're doing.

THE WRITE STUFF: PUTTING YOUR IDEAS ON PAPER

Before your eager audience can come together in a darkened theater[3] and partake in the cinematic genius that is your very own damn movie, one really important thing has to happen first: you need to have a story to tell. This may sound painfully obvious, but judging by the quality of films playing at the average multiplex, most studio pictures seem to go from start to finish without any consideration to story at all. I remember sitting in the audience at a screening of *Lethal Weapon 4* and thinking "this makes absolutely no sense! It's as if they just made the entire movie up as they went along." Later, I would find out that they pretty much did exactly that.

As a director, the story that you choose to bring to life should challenge your audience. It should be the kind of story that they leave the theater talking about, a story that they could quite possibly get into an argument with their best of friends over. If you manage to evoke such a strong emotional response from your audience while also telling a story that is meaningful and important to you, then congratulations! You will have accomplished more with your

---

[3]As opposed to having your audience cum together in a darkened theater. See *Strap on Sally Part 13*. Now there's a focused screenplay.

storytelling abilities than 99% of the garbage that Hollywood is currently churning out. Notice that I said that the story has to be meaningful to YOU above all else. After all, if the story doesn't interest *you*, how in the hell can you expect it to interest anyone else?

GETTING INTO DIRECTING . . . RON JEREMY STYLE

Ron Jeremy is an icon of the adult film world and the self-proclaimed "hardest (working) man in showbiz." Lloyd respects that, but would like to formally challenge Ron to defend that title. Preferably in a nice men's room somewhere out on Highway 95.

FIGURE 2.2 Lloyd Kaufman takes a ride on Ron Jeremy.

The way you break into directing porn is usually just to shoot your own scene. It's not like a mainstream movie. The funny thing is porn has led the way to most new technology. The first prerecorded cassettes, CD-ROMs, DVDs, and hi-definition were porn. And obviously the Internet was pretty much infiltrated by porn. So porn is actually one of the leaders in technology because it's already an experimental medium. You couldn't tell a guy in the mainstream to get a camera and just go out and film people. You need a storyline and other things.

In porn, though, you can shoot your friends having sex, or you having sex. Have a friend of yours as a camera man. Shoot it, have your friends shoot you and your date, or you shoot a couple. Get a lot of nice angles. Make it look pretty hot and passionate. Have some nice scenery, maybe a lovely bedroom, maybe a nice view out the window and then you bring that to an adult company. Maybe they'll buy the scene from you, and if they like it, they'll give you more. The addresses of all the adult companies are on the side of the DVD boxes. You can contact a company and say "I've got a great thing that I shot, may I show it to you?" Or you can go to a tradeshow, like a Ms. January super-electronics show at the The Adult Entertainment Expo (AEE), and you go to all the various companies, who are all right there under one roof. Make a lot of dupes of your scene and put a line through it saying "for screening purposes only." You go to all the various companies; Vivid, Wicked, ECA, Hustler, Metro, etc., and you give them your tape and say, "if you like it, I'd like to shoot more porn." That's how you can get a job directing porn.

A NOTE ON FORMATTING

The average movie script is formatted in a very specific manner, resulting in an average of one page being one minute on screen. Fortunately, this isn't an average script we are talking about here. This is YOUR script. Therefore, it is entirely up to you if you want to follow the standard script format or not. There are pros and cons to sticking to this format.

I should probably tell you that the whole "one page per minute" thing usually gets tossed right out the window on a Troma movie. Truth be told, we often average two minutes a page, if not more. Because of this, we try to keep our scripts as short as possible. If you are planning on maintaining full control and directing your own script (which is probably why you bought this book), then your script can be in any damn format you choose.

However, since there already exists an industry standard for scripts, you might as well take the time to learn how to format your script so that it adheres to this standard. Luckily for you there are a wide variety of software programs available that will guide you through the entire process. Programs such as Movie Magic Screenwriter, Script Buddy, and Final Draft are among the more popular software packages on the market. If you're really broke, you can look up the proper script format online and tab and center your heart out on your word processor.[4]

---

[4]Satisfied? Word processor is the current lingo, right?

I HAVE AN IDEA, NOW WHAT?

So it finally happened. The beautiful, topless pixie known as inspiration has bared her perky little boobies[5] to your brain and now you want to get your ideas down on paper as quickly as possible. Of course, talking about your script is the easy part. Coffee shops are full of young hipsters going on and on about the script they are working on.[6] So why aren't they at home writing instead of sipping Grande Soy Mocha Cappuccinos? I'll tell you why — because sitting down and hammering the damn thing out is a gigantic pain in the ass. But it's a pain you will learn to endure, and eventually, embrace. Who knows, maybe you will be so driven with inspiration that you will knock it out over a weekend, or maybe you will need to be pushed and prodded the entire time.*

Some writers prefer to work under a strictly enforced self-imposed deadline. If this appeals to you, I suggest you shoot for around five pages a day. The point here is to get those words on paper as rapidly as possible so you can fiddle around with them later on. If you're more of a lazy-ass, you will probably be best served by working on your script whenever you run out of Cheese Doodles and Hot Pockets. Just get the damn thing written!

Remember, as a Writer/Director, you can count yourself among the company of cinematic giants! In 1965, Woody Allen wrote *What's New Pussycat?* and was appalled when the producers of the film took it and rearranged it entirely. He vowed from that point on to never write another script unless he was going to direct it himself. Now that's what I call dedication to your vision! It is rumored that Woody Allen went on to write three scripts in a single weekend. I, on the other hand, once *read* three scripts in a single weekend. Okay, it was only two.

---

[5]This is a completely politically correct book, so any gynos reading this, feel free to insert "penis" here instead of "boobies." Any men reading this footnote, feel free to insert penis anywhere you would like. I do.

[6]At least, that's what they tell me. The closest thing to a coffee shop around Troma's new Long Island City office is Gus's Deli, which occasionally serves coffee, and has one table in front of the soda cooler, which is usually occupied by elderly Cubans discussing the next hurricane.

*LONELY FOOTNOTE GUY SAYS: If anyone needs to be poked or prodded, I'm available. Just send a message and a picture to my Myspace, myspace.com/chickenzombie.

It is vitally important that you not fall into the trap of the "masterpiece syndrome." This is when you find yourself continuously revising your script and never actually get around to finishing it, not to mention shooting it. As my grandmother was always fond of saying, "fuck that noise!" You can always tweak and change your script later on during the shooting. In the same vein, if you're having trouble even beginning, just get something down. You can't edit a blank page.

If you find that you just don't have the time to get your script written on your own, you can wrangle a cowriter to help you out. I have had cowriters on every single Troma film I have written and directed, and they came out just fine!* If this is the route you choose to take, you can come up with an idea, write a thorough synopsis with key scenes and dialogue that you want included, and hand it off to someone else to write it all out for you. You can then take this first draft and begin to re-work it as you see fit. Unless, of course, your cowriter just happens to be named Herman J. Mankiewicz,[7] in which case you're better off not changing a goddamned word.

For someone without a lot of time on his hands but who has a great story to tell, this situation may be ideal. When the film is complete, credit the screenplay as being by your cowriter and yourself, based on an original story by you. That way everyone gets due credit and no feelings get hurt. The last thing you want to do is screw someone out of his or her proper recognition for contributing to your film.[8]

If you're a deranged control freak such as myself, you will be obsessively involved in every step of the story process from the get-go. But what if someone comes to you with a script that they have written entirely themselves? Well, if it's a story that you want to tell, then by all means do it. Hopefully you will be able to make your personal imprint on the film, creating a work that reflects your personal style of filmmaking.

---

*EDITOR'S NOTE: To my knowledge, there is nothing "fine" about anything Lloyd Kaufman has done.

[7]Cowriter of the seldom-seen, underground sensation known as *Citizen Kane*.

[8]This does not apply to books, Sara and Kurly . . .

BREATHING LIFE INTO THE STORY, AS YOU WOULD A DROWNING KITTEN

Some writers will have the entire ending to their film in mind before they even set pen to paper. That way, they have a definite destination to guide their characters to. Others will have an idea for their story, but have no idea how it's going to end. They find that the story somehow "writes itself" and that the characters take on a life of their own and guide the narrative. Whatever method you choose is fine, as long as it works for you.

The characters in your film can be rough archetypes, flat-out stereotypes, based on people you know in real life, or carefully devised from scratch. I have heard of some writers actually writing full biographies for each of their characters, including every aspect of their lives up until just before the time frame of the film. These biographies can then be handed off to the actors so they can better get into character. This sounds like too much damn work to me, but if it sounds appealing to you then go for it.

What is important is that you are completely aware of your character's backgrounds and motivations so that they always act accordingly within the confines of your story. If you have them behaving completely out of character halfway through the film, you'll confuse and piss off your audience.

A LOCATION IS ALWAYS BETTER (AND OFTEN CHEAPER) THAN A SET

All too often, I have seen young filmmakers make the mistake of overlooking many of the valuable resources which exist around them, ripe for the taking. This is a tragic error. If you or a friend happens to own or have access to a unique prop or location, you should make every effort to include it in your film. Does your toothless half-cousin Maynard drive a semi-truck? Then put a semi-truck driving pedophile priest in the script! You say gay cousin Billy is the manager of a tranny strip-club? You bet your ass you better include it in your story! In fact, you should take inventory of everything readily available to you that could add production value to your film and include as much of it in your script as possible.

At Troma we always ask our actors if they have any interesting abilities or deformities so that we can include them in the movie.

If you happen to find out that your female lead is also an incredibly talented sword-swallowing contortionist halfway through your shoot, re-work the script to allow her to show off those skills (and ask her out on a date, you idiot!) In short, take advantage of every opportunity to increase the "uniqueness factor" of your movie.

With that said, under no circumstances whatsoever should you limit the scope of your story based on your lack of physical or monetary resources. Do you need to blow up a building to make your story work? Then put it in the damn script! A resourceful filmmaker will figure out how to get it done. We needed to blow up an entire school for *Citizen Toxie* and we managed to pull it off quite nicely for around five bucks![9] Let there be no barriers to your creativity.

Recently, my good friend and fellow independent producer, Roger Corman,[10] let me in on a problem he had with a film called *Cyclops* that he made for the Sci-Fi channel. The film was originally supposed to take place on a boring, desolate old island. Not happy with the location, Roger remembered a story he had read about a fantastic, unused Spartacus set in Eastern Europe (Bulgaria, or Italy or something. Hell, they are practically the same place anyway). Roger quickly secured the Spartacus set and re-worked his script to take advantage of this incredible new location. The Cyclops would attack ancient Rome — much better than some shitty, boring, deserted island. What could have been a big nothing was transformed into an excellent opportunity. Roger Corman didn't allow outside limitations to hinder his style, and he wound up with a far better look for his film as a result of his determination and vision.

From what I hear the Sci-Fi channel has a laundry list full of obnoxious rules telling filmmakers how they want their movies made. If I remember correctly, the name of the monster has to appear in the title of the film, the monster has to appear within the first five minutes, there has to be a death every eight minutes, and

---

[9]You can see how we pulled this off by watching *Apocalypse Soon: The Making Of Citizen Toxie*, available right now on DVD at www.troma.com. BUY TROMA!

[10]Roger Corman directed many classics such as *The Trip, Man with the X-Ray Eyes, Little Shop of Horrors* (shot in 2 days on 35 mm film!), and has discovered just about every prominent actor and filmmaker of our time from Jack Nicholson to Francis Ford Coppola to Jonathan Demme to Martin Scorsese. In a fair world he would have won two lifetime achievement Oscars, but because he is an independent producer/director he has sadly won none.

no shots are to take place at night. I don't know about you, but this list sounds like a step-by-step recipe for one shitty horror film. With rules like this it's no wonder that nearly all the Sci-Fi channel's movies are turds. Don't let this discourage you from making a film for the Sci-Fi channel should the opportunity arise, because, like Roger Corman, you too can turn chicken shit into chicken salad. In fact some of the best films ever made were originally intended to be schlocko, potboiler, second bills on a double feature. Occasionally, geniuses like Joseph H. Lewis (*Gun Crazy*) and Edgar G. Ulmer (*Black Cat*) come onto the scene, satisfy the requirements of hack movie executives, and still manage to create masterpieces. You can do the same.

WRITING AND RE-WRITING

All too often, filmmakers make the fatal error of thinking that their scripts are written in stone. That if it doesn't appear on the page, then it can't appear on the screen. Of course, this is complete bullshit. Your script is there to guide you — to get your story told and onto the screen. And since it's YOUR story, you get to decide which transmutations and transfigurations it will undergo. This may come as a shock, but you won't be shipped off to "movie jail" for constantly re-writing and changing the script. Hell, on a Troma movie it's not uncommon to change lines of dialogue in between takes. And a Troma set is kind of like movie jail anyway, so there you go!

Your script is like a malleable hunk of clay, and you're the artist. Feel free to experiment and be open to improvisations and suggestions from the actors and the rest of your crew. A quick thinking director knows opportunity when she sees it, and will alter her script as conditions allow. For example, if you live near a beach and a whale just so happens to wash up onto the shore, you could take full advantage of this misfortune and include footage of the tragedy in your film.[11] Your main character might partake in the rescue effort, the whale could be a sign from God, or you could have your main villain savagely rape the poor creature right there on the beach — onlookers be damned. The possibilities are endless!

---

[11]Plus you would have a great homage to the disgustingly weird and bloated fish that washes up on the beach in the final scene of Fellini's *La Dolce Vita!*

During the shooting of the *Stink of Flesh*, an incredible independent zombie film starring one of my cowriters Kurly Tlapoyawa, the cast and crew reacted quickly to a sudden rainstorm in the New Mexico desert. They dropped everything and quickly ran outside to film the arrival of a group of wounded soldiers. The dark clouds hovering above, combined with the pelting rain and bolts of lightning streaking across the sky behind the soldiers, added instant production value. A lesser crew would have waited inside until the rain stopped before they continued shooting.[12] The important thing is to respond to these opportunities quickly. If you waste too much time mulling over your options, the chance may pass you by. Motion always beats meditation.

COLORS THAT DON'T RESULT IN DRIVE-BYS

As changes to your script are made, the latest, newest versions of the pages should be printed out on different colored paper and inserted into everyone's script so people will understand that revisions are being distributed. It helps if you use a different color of paper to denote the latest version of each change (version one changes are yellow, version two are blue, and so on). Sounds simple, right? Well, on the set of *Citizen Toxie*, we had a young PA who just couldn't seem to wrap her brain around this concept, and infuriated me with her inability to comprehend the procedure. I had her shot and buried just outside of New Jersey.[13]

YOU COULD PUT AN EYE OUT WITH THAT THING!

The only times I feel it's acceptable to rigidly adhere to your script are when it comes to stunts and special effects shots.[14] These should always be carefully planned out in advance, storyboarded, and rehearsed in as much painstaking detail as possible prior

---

[12]Of course, two soldiers and a donkey were all struck by lightning, but no one ever said filmmaking was easy.

[13]Okay, so we didn't have her shot. But it sounded cool. The point is, on low-budget movies you must have patience for young hardworking people who are inexperienced . . . and at times, dense.

[14]Or when arguing the artistic integrity of nudity with a young gyno-American who has chosen to change her mind at the last minute regarding her full frontal "wrestling in tapioca pudding" scene.

to shooting. You want to make sure that your stunts are going to be pulled off safely, especially if you're shooting a no-budget film and can't afford any insurance (any waivers you get signed by your actors promising that they won't sue the hell out of you if they catch a nail in their eye are pretty much worthless, no matter how well worded they may be).

Special effects shots also need to be planned out and rehearsed as early on and as frequently as possible. You don't want to wait until the day of your big bridge collapse sequence to find out that the construction paper and firecrackers mock-up you hastily assembled at the last minute just isn't going to cut it. By carefully preparing and planning these shots, you help diminish the possibility of losing valuable shooting time just because something isn't working out as you had hoped.*

NUMBERING YOUR SCENES

With your script now complete, you need to go through it page by page and number every single one of your scenes. This will ensure that you get everything you need shot on any given day, and will aid you greatly in creating your shooting schedule. Hence, this is called your "shooting script." As you shoot each scene, be sure to make any notes you may need on this script, and to mark off the scenes as you shoot them. This marked-up script with scenes numbered will also become your editor's Bible. Unless he's a Buddhist.

THE POOR MAN'S COPYRIGHT[15]

Once you have the first version of your script completed, you should print it out, throw it into a large manila envelope, sign your name across the seal, and mail it to yourself via registered mail. When it arrives at your home, store it in a safe place. If some asshole tries to rip you off, you now have a piece of registered mail, dated and

---

*EDITOR'S NOTE: Lloyd, you do have a whole chapter devoted to preproduction coming up, and then another one devoted to special effects. Shouldn't we save this for either of those?

LLOYD'S RESPONSE: Don't worry. I'm sure I'll be repeating myself quite a bit.

[15]Personally, I don't worry about being ripped off. I consider it a compliment, and I'm sure that the people I have ripped off over the years feel the same way. But I get asked about this issue quite often, so I figured I would throw it in to take up some room.

stamped, to prove that the content of the script is your intellectual property. Just never open the damn thing or you will have gone through all that work for nothing.

Keep in mind, this is a filmmaking book and not intended to be legitimate legal advice of any sort. If it turns out that this doesn't hold up in court, you only have yourself to blame for listening to a pathetic old Jew who makes movies about giant zombie chickens and hard-bodied lesbians. In other words, don't go crying to your lawyer if this doesn't work. In fact, forget I mentioned it at all; just go get a proper copyright for Christ's sake!

FIGURE 2.3 *Jason Yachanin (Arbie) and Lloyd Kaufman (Old Arbie) share a private moment while rehearsing their beautiful and sentimental song and dance number on the set of* Poultrygeist.

ENTER THE COWRITER

Personally, I find it much easier to find a cowriter to help me speed the project along. I usually come up with an idea based on some personal experience I have had (lots of McDonald's plastic containers and cups strewn throughout the countryside during family camping trips helped to birth *The Toxic Avenger*, while fighting giant rats we inherited from the McDonald's next door in the basement of the

Troma building with a shovel inspired *Poultrygeist*)[16] and then I will usually write out a synopsis or a short treatment and find some hot, young individual to write it all out with me. I choose to work this way for three reasons:

1. A younger person tends to be much more of a shit-disturber than I am, and will make sure that I don't make any compromises.
2. Having a writing partner will tend to get me more focused on the task at hand.
3. I'm old and lazy.*

In fact, I have only written one feature-length script entirely on my own. It was in 1970 and based on a story line given to me by Stan Lee called *Night of the Witch.* As much as I hated to do it, I sat in front of that damned typewriter and grinded the entire thing out, page by painstaking page. Since then I decided it would be much easier to do what Stan just did, come up with a thorough idea, and then bring in someone else to help me along with it. In fact, I did that with this very book! I developed a complete outline for the book, and then brought in two incredibly talented and fantastic cowriters[17] to go about bringing that outline to life. It's a collaborative effort, which, I feel, pays off in the end. Plus, I get to make them do all of the really boring shit, like proofreading meye horribl tieping.[18]

AND NOW A FEW WORDS FROM KURLY

It's a nice brisk Saturday morning. I'm hard at work at Burning Paradise Video world headquarters, located in the heart of downtown Albuquerque, New Mexico. There is a gigantic stack of DVDs waiting to be checked back in, an in-box of work I need to get done piled a mile high on my desk, and approximately half a million unread e-mails staring back at me from my computer monitor. My name is Kurly Tlapoyawa, welcome to my life.

---

[16] Wow, I guess I actually owe a lot to McDonald's. Thanks for being so dirty guys!

*EDITOR'S NOTE: Kurly and Sara both wanted me to put this statement in bold, but I thought that might be in bad taste.

[17] Wow, can you guess who wrote this line?

[18] Again, any guesses on who wrote this part? I'll give you a hint . . . it wasn't me.

Not that I'm complaining, mind you. I just get a little overwhelmed sometimes.

"Fuck it," I decide. "I'm not taking on any extra work until I get my shit in order."

The phone rings.

"Thank you for calling Burning Paradise."

"Kurly, It's Lloyd. How are you?"

"Fine Lloyd, how the hell are you?"

"Good, good. How is the weather over there?"

"Cold."

"Great, great. Anyway, I need a cowriter for my new book."

". . ."

"You still there?"

"Yes Lloyd, I sure am."

"You want the job?"

At this point a million things are racing through my mind. I should know better. I have enough on my plate as it is. Plus, I have heard the horror stories of having Lloyd as a boss. There is simply no way I can say yes. But still . . . My name on a Lloyd Kaufman book — Wow!

"What do you have in mind, Lloyd?"

"Well, you should know right off the bat that there is very little money in this, like none whatsoever. And we need to work fast."

"How fast?"

"Like yesterday fast."

"I don't know Lloyd. I'm pretty busy."

"Of course, of course. But think of the benefits you would get from doing this. The possibilities it will create for you. Look, all I need you to do is read over what I write and see if you can bring a fresh, young perspective to it all. It will be easy."

I pause for a moment, thinking about my options. Lloyd is absolutely right. The man is a living legend for Christ's sake; I would have to be half a retard to turn this opportunity down.*

"Fuck it. I'm in."

"Fantastic! I'm e-mailing you the first chapter right now. I need any suggestions and additions you may have for me by Tuesday."

"That's in three days, Lloyd."

---

*KURLY SAYS: Lloyd wrote that.

"I realize that, but time is of the essence. There's this editor named Elinor and she's pretty tough . . ."

"Fine. I'll get started right away."

"Thanks."

And with that I continued my lifelong tradition of biting off way more than I can possibly chew. Of course, I had no idea what to expect from this little arrangement, so I decided to give my good buddy and Troma alumni Trent Haaga a call and see if he had any words of advice to share.

"Trent, it's Kurly."

"Hey Kurly, wassup?"

"Well, it looks like I'm working on Lloyd's new book."

" . . ."

"Trent, you still there?"

"Yeah, I'm here."

"So what do you think?"

"Did you already sign the contract?"

"Well, not yet."

"Run."

"What?"

"Run. Get out of it."

"I can't do that man. I gave him my word I would do it."

"Wow," Trent says. "Congratulations . . . and I'm sorry."

"Sorry? Sorry about what?"

"You'll find out soon enough."

And there you have it. What started out as a normal, mundane day at Burning Paradise transformed into a project that I hadn't anticipated doing at all. But did I shy away from the challenge? Hell no! I grabbed my nuts and jumped right into the fire. Such is the "can do" attitude you will need when embarking on your own filmmaking journey.

AND NOW, BACK TO LLOYD

Actually, Kurly makes it sound a lot worse than it really is. I just so happen to know that working with me is one of the easiest and enjoyable things a person could do. Just ask Sara — she's here every day! I'm a joy to work with — trust me.

Keep in mind that even with a cowriter at your side, your script may take a shit-ton of time to finish. In fact, I went through five different cowriters on *Tromeo & Juliet* and still wasn't satisfied with the end result. It wasn't until I collaborated with James Gunn that I

FIGURE 2.4 *Lloyd Kaufman and Trent Haaga watch the latest atomic bomb test blast in Nevada.*

found the script I was looking for. In the end it took several years to arrive at the script I felt truly delivered the story I wanted to tell.

The exact opposite is true regarding the script for *Poultrygeist*. It was while dealing with the rat infestation in the basement of the old Troma building (courtesy of the newly opened McDonald's next door to us) that intrepid 10-year Troma employee and fellow fast-food hater Gabe Friedman and I birthed the initial idea for the story. Drawing upon Gabe's years of experience slinging burgers at various fast-food joints, coupled with my hatred of corporate America and love for hard-bodied lesbians, we dove into the script at full speed. Together we managed to knock out a solid first draft in no time flat, resulting in what I feel is the best Troma film ever made.

Of course, if you don't work well with others, I would suggest you stay away from this work model and just write the entire damn thing on your own. Some folks, like Woody Allen, have set strict goals for themselves when it comes to writing, grinding out a set number of pages each day, whether they feel inspired to or not. This will at least get a first draft of the script done, and then you can set about tweaking and re-working it from there. The main point is to get your damn script written!

FIGURE 2.5 Eli Roth making the hand gestures of a true director. Or telling you that he is going to kick your ass . . .

You can make yourself crazy thinking about all of the technicalities, but don't. Do it. If you have that idea in your head that's the idea that won't let you sleep because you see it every time you close your eyes, if you literally have insomnia because there's a voice poking you going, "Do it. Shoot it. Shoot it." Go for it. Make your film, but make it great. Shoot like every day is the last day of your life, like your fucking life depends on it. Say "let's put as much as we can into the story, into the acting, into the production design . . . let's just fucking go for it". And make something great. Put something awesome out there, even if it's a really sick, fucked-up, violent horror film, do it. Make it better than anybody else ever has before.

LET'S GET CRACKING!

So there you have it, a down and dirty Tromatic primer on getting your script written and ready for production. So now go get that damn script written and I'll meet you in the next chapter to continue this madness. Don't worry; I'll wait for you.

Chapter three

Show, Don't Tell, and Other Things My Uncle Lance Whispered to Me in the Basement

Finished writing that amazing script already? Great! Now that you have an incredible and inspiring story to tell, you need to figure out a way to bring it to life in a visually compelling style. Far too many films suffer from uninspired shots and a complete lack of visual flair. These films are known as Troma movies. This, however, won't be the case with your film! No dear reader, your movie will be a visually orgasmic event, imbued with such passion and creativity that Martin Scorsese[1] himself will be begging you for advice. Of course, if this winds up not being the case, you can always get your movie distributed by Troma. That way you will at least have a copy of your film on DVD to clutch in your masturbatory-crippled hands while you cry yourself

---

[1]Martin Scorsese is arguably America's most revered modern day director. He has inspired a tsunami of self conscious, pretentious "look at me, I'm a director" film school graduates.

to sleep at night because your significant other left you for the cable repairman. But hey, you will never know until you try it!

THE "EYES" HAVE IT!

This may seem like an obvious statement to make, but filmmaking is a visual medium. It is your job as director to bring your character's motives, fears, and accomplishments to the screen in a visual manner, not through reams of mind-numbing dialogue. This is not to say that dialogue is not important, but you're making a movie here, not writing a novel. Think about it, would you rather watch a couple of guys standing around talking about the crazy, sex-filled, she-male midget and circus clown orgy that they threw the night before, or would you rather see it all go down first-hand? That's what I thought. Incidentally, if your movie actually happens to contain a sex-filled, she-male midget and circus clown orgy, let me know. I twist a mean balloon animal.*

MAKING MISTAKES . . . RON JEREMY STYLE

I've directed a lot of adult movies, and I think one of the biggest mistakes directors make is talking too much. If you want your actors to get into the groove, it kind of takes some of the fun away from it when your director's going, "Okay, move your leg, okay now, smile more." The best thing a director can do in an adult movie is shut the hell up.

There are two common directions I use in porn. One is to "undulate" and often the girls don't know what it means. Pop your body! Even though she can be moving her head back and forth, if we go in for a close up on the torso and it's not moving, the whole thing doesn't look that exciting. I also tell people to smile more. I want a lot of smiling. A girl can have an orgasmic face and it might look good or feel good, but some people could misconstrue it as painful. In porn we want people to be enjoying themselves. Smiling faces, ear to ear.

Another mistake porn directors make is when an actor says he's having a bit of trouble, you know, getting wood and a director puts on the pressure. The director says, "Nick, hey c'mon we're losing daylight. You gotta get this thing going, get that purple headed soldier at attention mister, we gotta GO, c'mon MOVE IT, MOVE IT, MOVE IT!" It's not going to help. If an actor is feeling

---

*A NOTE FROM YOUR FRIENDLY FOOTNOTE GUY: I'm feeling a little left out. Does anyone want to chat? My screen name is smallprintluver.

pressure, nothing is going to happen. Make your actor feel really relaxed. Just enjoy, hug, kiss, cuddle, caress — we've got plenty of time. Take the pressure OFF the actor and he'll get a nice boner.

Another common mistake that directors make, and this is downright funny . . . I'll say this delicately. I don't know why, since this is for Lloyd, but I'll be delicate. You're doing an anal sex scene and the girl is afraid that she's just had a big meal earlier that day . . .*

The Editrix says: Sorry, guys, we can't print the rest of this sidebar — we really had to draw a line somewhere, and this is it . . .

My first feature film was essentially a crash-course in the art of visual story telling. You see, I shot my first film (*The Girl Who Returned*) on a Bolex — an amazing 16 mm camera that has no ability to shoot sync sound. This meant that I was essentially shooting a feature-length silent film, and had to add the music and narration manually in postproduction. Because of this, I was forced to focus on telling the story visually, rather than relying entirely on dialogue to carry the narrative flow. I still managed to make a very

*FOOTNOTE GUY SAYS: Hey Lloyd, I know you're probably pretty mad about this part of Ron Jeremy's sidebar being censored. Believe me, I didn't want to do it! I believe in freedom of speech as much as the next guy. But Lloyd, they offered to promote me if I went along with it. It was a lot of money, and well, that part of the sidebar was pretty graphic . . . As part of my apology, though, I will put this plug in for you — If anyone wants to see the complete Ron Jeremy interview, check out the *Direct Your Own Damn Movie* Box Set, available now from www.troma. com. BUY TROMA!! (Are we okay, Lloyd? I hope you don't hold it against me. I love you . . .)

ponderous and boring film. I recommend that you take the time to watch some of the great silent films of our time such as *The Last Laugh* by von Sternberg, *Häxan* by Benjamin Christensen, and any of D.W. Griffith and Charlie Chaplin's films as a primer in the craft of visual storytelling.

A good way to tell if your story works visually is to watch it with the volume level turned all the way down. If your main character's heart-breaking confession to his wife comes off as him telling her a dick and fart joke when the sound is off, you might just want to tweak the way you shot it or edited it. Remember, you want your actors to convey their innermost thoughts through action, tone, and expression. If your hero has issues with another character, have him show it by punching his nemesis in the nuts. This will get your point across in a far more exciting and compelling fashion than by having him say "Gee, I hate that guy."

STYLES OF STORYTELLING

There is no school called "go here and we guarantee to make you a great director." In fact, many of the greatest directors to ever live have had wildly different styles. I consider Andy Warhol to be one of the true greats, and he shot a 35-minute film of a man sleeping. I once shot a film[2] that put the entire audience to sleep in less than 35 minutes. Cinematic giants such as John Ford and Otto Preminger had very different styles and approaches to shooting a film, yet they are both incredible directors. Remember, just like writing a script, there are no step-by-step rules to directing a film. If a particular method works for you and your peeps,[3] then use it.

Some directors seem to thrive on a Gonzo approach to filmmaking. Giuseppe Andrews,[4] for example, is a true auteur who utilizes a very fast and loose approach to his films. He makes his

---

[2] *The Battle of Loves Return*; it introduced a revolutionary way to save money. The movie was only 75 minutes long, but it was so boring it seemed like 95 minutes. Sorry about that. It also introduced Oliver Stone to the world. Sorry about that too.

[3] I use the term "peeps" not because I'm hip like that, but because I have been incapable of completing a sentence without using some kind of chicken pun since 2005.

[4] His day job is acting in films like *Cabin Fever, Detroit Rock City*, etc., but his real love is filmmaking.

feature-length movies completely guerilla style and on a budget of about $1000 per film. He doesn't use professional actors, and often functions entirely as a one-man production crew. His movies are brilliant. Along a similar vein, Howard Hawks was notorious for waiting until the last possible second before shooting to decide how he was going to pull off a particular scene. His movies are also brilliant. Alfred Hitchcock, on the other hand, was a complete control freak — overseeing every single aspect of production. He carefully sketched out every scene far in advance, and knew exactly how they were to be accomplished. It's rumored that Alfred Hitchcock didn't even look in the camera while shooting a scene. His work ethic and preparation were so meticulous that he felt he didn't need to. His movies define "brilliant." They also define "perverse."

Personally, I think I fall in the middle of these two extremes (minus the part about being brilliant). I prefer to be as well prepared as possible when going into production. In fact, I often run and videotape full dress rehearsals at the actual locations far in advance of filming. In this sense I am like Hitchcock. But I am also completely open to improvisations and suggestions from my cast and crew. The way I see it, by maintaining a certain level of flexibility, I'm afforded more opportunities for good ideas to sneak their way into my movies (and Lord knows they don't make it in on purpose).

A good example of this principle in action is Jason Yachanin, the outstanding young actor who played the role of Arbie in *Poultrygeist*. Throughout production, Jason came up with numerous ad-libbed lines and actions which worked out incredibly well. For example, when Arbie and another character enter a heinously defiled men's room after Joe Fleishaker shits himself inside-out, it was Jason's idea to pick up Joe's feces-encased shoe and sniff it out of curiosity. The disgust that the audience feels by the sight of the brown Jackson Pollock-esque wall of human excrement is counter-balanced by sheer comedic brilliance! Jason also came up with the idea of shouting out "You're so hot, I just want to fuck you!" when the Muslim character Humus strips off her burqa, revealing a smoking hot body with an IED strapped to it. Had I been even more of a hard-ass than I usually am, I would have admonished him for doing these things on the fly, ultimately losing out on some great bits.

A QUICK PRIMER ON THINGS THAT I WILL REPEAT IN THE COMING CHAPTERS

While working on *Rocky*, I learned from director John G. Avildsen[5] to try to shoot in sequence. This, John pointed out, would allow him to re-write and restructure the film as he went along. This is a lesson I took to heart and follow to this very day. Apart from sex scenes (which I usually shoot first to avoid having my actors get cold feet — or rather cold nether regions — and chicken out on me later on down the line), I shoot my films entirely in sequence. This gives me way more flexibility in shaping the course of the film than shooting out of sequence ever could.

While making *The Toxic Avenger, Part II*, the jerk-off* who was playing Toxie decided he was now a mega-superstar and started strutting around the set, acting like a spoiled diva. I fired him two weeks into production and had him replaced by a taller, more muscular guy. Both actors wore the Toxie mask, so who was going to notice? If I had been shooting out of sequence, we would have wound up with a pretty obvious on-screen discrepancy when Toxie's body changed from scene to scene — i.e. we would see Toxie getting smaller and larger then smaller again. By shooting in sequence, there was only one change in Toxie's magnitude. I kept the look of Toxie fairly consistent in terms of continuity, at least from the point of replacing the original actor.

I think one of the worst mistakes a director can make is to shoot the end of the film first. This would greatly restrict the flow of your film, as every scene prior to that point has to be leading to that particular ending. If you get a brilliant new idea or suddenly decide that your hero no longer needs to rape puppies to get your point across halfway through your shoot, you're simply out of luck. Shooting your ending first is a good way to paint yourself into a corner. When I appeared in *Orgazmo* I was told by Trey Parker[6] that the scene we were shooting was the last scene in the movie. This, incidentally, was the first day of filming on the entire movie.

---

[5] John also directed *Cry Uncle*, available now from www.troma.com. BUY TROMA!

*EDITOR'S NOTE: Do you remember who this actor was? We may need to get clearance from our legal department if you insist on calling him a jerk-off . . .

[6] Trey Parker and Matt Stone created the somewhat successful children's show *South Park*. Their first film, *Cannibal! The Musical* is available now from www.troma.com. BUY TROMA!!

FIGURE 3.1 *Toxic Avenger, circa September 10, 2001.*

"Are you sure you want to shoot the ending first?" I asked Trey.

"Don't worry about it Lloyd," he responded. "This is the exact ending I want. In fact, it sets up the sequel."

Even though this decision exhibited complete confidence in Trey's storytelling abilities, I still think he made a fatal error by shooting the ending first. And as predicted, his career has floundered and gone absolutely nowhere since making *Orgazmo*, while I remain firmly entrenched among the Hollywood elite. In fact, I truly believe that I owe my incredible success as a director to having always shot my films in sequence. If you are ever on Hollywood Boulevard late at night and Trey happens to offer you a game of "anonymous hands" in a filthy men's room stall, slide him a few extra bucks and tell him that Lloyd wishes him well.* Poor bastard.**

LOCATION, LOCATION, LOCATION

I highly recommend that you, whenever possible, use actual locations as opposed to building sets to shoot on. An actual bar is always going to look better than a fake one,[7] and things such as fake graveyards just look cheesy and ridiculous. By using actual locations, you bring an unmatched feeling of authenticity into your movie. This is because a location will always have a better on-screen aesthetic than a fake one. Basically, a good location will become a character in the film. Also, a real location allows you to keep one foot in reality, and this is of utmost importance if you're shooting a movie with a fantastic premise. By grounding at least one aspect of your movie in reality, you make the movie far more believable.

There is a scene in *The Toxic Avenger Part III: The Last Temptation of Toxie* that takes place in a video store. Toxie does some implausible things like disembowel and jump rope with a dude's guts. He forces a bad guy's hands into the VCR and they are miraculously projected onto the TV screen as they get mangled up by

---

*EDITOR'S NOTE to Trey Parker: Kaufman seems to think this joke is funny. Focal Press and its parent company, Reed Elsevier, don't share his opinion. If you decide to sue anyone, please don't sue us. We are going to lose enough money on this book as it is.

**A NOTE FROM YOUR BORED YET FRIENDLY FOOTNOTE GUY: I'd like to send a message to Trey Parker too! Dear Trey, I'm all alone here at the office. If you come over, I'll buzz you up. Please come over . . .

[7]And when no one is looking, you can sneak some actual booze instead of that tea they use as liquor on studio sets.

FIGURE 3.2 *Lloyd Kaufman is given a rare opportunity to film Jackson Pollock as Museum of Modern Art staff discreetly observe.*

the gears of the machine. Another guy's face is erased on a bulk magnetic tape-erasing machine. Now, this scene might have been absolutely *ridiculous* without our realistic location. By using an actual video store, we not only saved money by not having to build a set, which would have looked like a fake video store, but we were able to have the visual credibility of a fully functioning video store serve as the background of a completely unrealistic scene. Incidentally, if you are ever in Albuquerque, New Mexico, you should swing by Burning Paradise Video, an amazing video store dedicated to the advancement of independent and foreign film. It is one of the few video stores in the nation that sports an entire Troma section. I have also heard rumors that the collection of she-male porn housed in the basement of Burning Paradise Video is quite impressive. You know that scene at the end of *Raiders of the Lost Ark*? You get the picture.*

NO COUNTRY FOR OLD JEWS

I recently took a break from toiling over the mighty tome of directorial wisdom you now hold in your hands to go out to dinner and a

*FOOTNOTE GUY SAYS: Um, where is this place? I could use some companionship right now . . .

FIGURE 3.3 *Indie film goddess Julie Strain and husband,* Teenage Mutant Ninja Turtles *creator Kevin Eastman, on the set of* Citizen Toxie *with a young Robert Redford* (center).

movie with my wife. And since Pattie-pie refuses to step foot in the Pussycat Theater to this very day, we settled on catching the ten o'clock show of *No Country For Old Men*. Now, for those of you who have been living in a cave in Pakistan for the last few years, *No Country For Old Men* is a very popular film directed by the Coen brothers and based on the award-winning novel written by Cormac McCarthy. Every film critic imaginable has ejaculated upon it with so much vigor that the film now resembles a young Asian woman in a Bukkake video. After the coming attractions had played, I sat in the darkened theater, my lips glossy from the buttery residue left by my gigantic bag of popcorn, and watched in amazement as the carnage unfolded on the big screen.

"Good Lord," I realized. "The Coen brothers have made an 80s slasher movie!" And mainstream movie-goers loved every minute of it.

If you have yet to see *No Country For Old Men*, you might want to skip this part of the book, since it contains "spoilers" as the kids like to say on the interweb message boards. In the film, the protagonist is hunted by a ruthless, unstoppable, wig-wearing killing machine, armed with a lethal vacuum cleaner and a rapist's wit. This guy is basically Michael Myers or Jason Voorhees, but without the mask and machete. The only thing missing was the adorable coed flashing her succulent breasts and fellating her boyfriend before meeting a grizzly end.

The Coen brothers are skilled filmmakers, no doubt. The film itself isn't terrible. In fact, I enjoyed it. The performances are good, the directing is good, and the New Mexico locations are dazzling. But it certainly isn't the best damn film ever made. What really chaps my ass-cheeks is the fact that *No Country For Old Men* utilizes filmmaking conventions that have been perfected by horror directors over the past thirty or so years, and as a result the film is being hailed as a work of cinematic genius. In contrast, filmmakers such as myself are looked down upon by these same critics, even though I helped CREATE the very techniques being used by the Coens.* But hey, I'm not bitter!

One major problem I had with *No Country For Old Men* was the complete lack of character development. We never really connect with the hero, and this lack of depth made me not really care whether he lived or died. The villain suits his purpose as the mysterious killer, but the hero should have had some sort of fleshing out to counterbalance this. If your audience can't connect with your main characters, you have a serious problem on your hands.**

I would venture to say that in the fullness of time, *Poultrygeist*, despite whatever flaws it may have, will be seen as a far better film than *No Country For Old Men*. It's certainly more personal a project

---

*SARA'S RESPONSE: I think you need to get over this. I really liked the movie. That part about some guy drinking another guy's milkshake was hilarious!

LLOYD'S RESPONSE: Don't be stupid. That milkshake line is from *Juno*. I think the toilet in my upstairs bedroom might be clogged. I need you to make some calls . . .

**EDITOR'S FOOTNOTE: Yes Lloyd, the Coens only made millions of dollars and won a few Oscars. That certainly sounds like a problem to me. Brilliant . . .

to me than *No Country* was to the Coen brothers, and I think it was more original and creative in its execution. Sure, on the surface *Poultrygeist* is the same old story of boy meets girl, boy loses girl to hard-bodied lesbian, boy gets girl back, and then everybody dies, but it also addresses some serious and relevant social issues.

Poultrygeist tackles problems such as racism, hypocrisy, chicken Indian zombies, corporate domination, bestiality, and the evils of the fast food industry, plus singing and dancing. *No Country For Old Men* had a guy in a wig hunting down a guy who found a lot of money. Hell, if I were to put out a movie tomorrow about a wig-wearing madman savagely cutting down his victims with a souped-up Flowbee, I sincerely doubt the critics would have given me the full-swallow blow job they have bestowed upon the Coens. Of course, *Poultrygeist* is a multiple Academy Award winning film, while the Coen brothers continue to languish in total obscurity, so I obviously came out on top here.

STUART GORDON ON DIRECTING HORROR

Stuart Gordon directed the horror classic Re-Animator, *and dipped his toes in another kind of horror as a writer on* Honey, I Shrunk the Kids. *While in college, he organized a stage production in which the aim was to get the audience to leave. He should have known that all he had to do was show Troma's masterpiece,* Big Gus, What's the Fuss?

Horror is a good way to start in this business. That was the advice that was given to me. Someone said the easiest movie to raise money for is the horror film and no matter how badly it turns out you'll probably be able to sell it to someone and your investors will get their money back. It's even truer today because horror is more popular than ever. I think that probably has something to do with 9/11. Audiences are flocking to see horror films.

One of the things I have learned is that horror is slow. Horror is about anticipation and the audience knowing that something bad is going to happen. Stretch that moment out as long as you possibly can. There are lots of shots in horror movies of people walking down hallways or opening doors or approaching bodies — those should be done slowly so that you really build up to something. The audience is just waiting for the horrific something or other to happen. John Carpenter says it's easy to scare someone, to make them jump, you know "boo," but it's the moments that lead up to that "boo" that really separate the men from the boys in terms of making horror films.

FIGURE 3.4 Stuart Gordon doing his famous Paul McCartney impersonation.

I've also learned that it is the little stuff that scares you the most. Godzilla destroying Tokyo is not scary, but a guy taking a razor blade and slicing the tip of his finger is terrifying. It is the things that we can relate to that make us cringe because we can imagine what this would be like. When things get too enormous it goes beyond human comprehension.

The other thing that is really important is having characters that the audience cares about. We really have to want to see these people survive. I'm not a big fan of the *Friday the 13th* movies where you have these obnoxious teenagers getting bumped off one by one because you're really on the side of Jason. You want to see those kids get it and so there is no real fear in those films at all. It just becomes a question of how they're going to die. With my first horror film, *Re-Animator*, there is a character, Herbert West, who is this guy who invented a serum that would bring the dead back to life. He was a really difficult character for the audience to really sympathize with — he's kind of a mad man. What we really needed in this story was a normal person to interact with him, so we created the character of his room-mate. We made this guy a poor kid who was at the University on a scholarship and dating the dean's daughter. He had all of these things going for him and all these things he could lose when he started teaming up with this crazy mad scientist. It made him very vulnerable and it made us really want to see him succeed.

I think the biggest mistake you can make is to censor yourself. I was making a film called *From Beyond*. I shot a sequence involving a woman being tortured and a big nail being pounded through her tongue, and ended up cutting it out of the movie myself because I thought there was no way that it would ever be allowed on screen. I thought, "Oh, that's the most disgusting thing in the world!" Now you walk around and you see all these women with pierced tongues, and it's exactly like what was I thinking. So that was a lesson to me. Don't ever do that.

THE TOOLS OF THE TRADE: YOUR FILMMAKING TOOL KIT

Well, you have your script, you have your cast and crew, and now you're ready to make a movie, right? Not so fast there, junior. There are a few items you'll need to throw together and learn how to use before you unleash your genius upon the unwashed masses. Luckily for you, I've put together a little laundry list of the essential film-making tools you will need on your journey. Here is a down and dirty list of the weapons you'll need:

Camera

This, of course, is the most crucial piece of equipment you'll need while making a movie. Without one of these, you're just shouting orders at people while they run around in costumes and take off their clothes. While that may sound like a perfectly reasonable way to spend your weekends, it's not making a movie. Fortunately, recent advancements in technology have made it easy to get a good digital camera at a fairly reasonable price.

Of course, I just so happen to be a Luddite with a fear of my own cell phone. Therefore, I stubbornly insist on shooting all of my features on 35 mm film. Since this option is probably way out of the price range for many of you reading this book, a digital video camera will do just fine. There are many different varieties of digital video cameras available. Whether they be 1 chip (the lowest image quality), 3 chip (broadcast quality), 24P (mimics film), or HD (the highest quality), I suggest that the budding filmmaker invest his money in a solid camera rather than spending it on film school. If you have the option of spending fifty grand on film school versus buying equipment, I say buy the damn equipment and start making movies. Some directors prefer to just hire a good DP, since they will have a pretty nice camera package[8] of their own. This can cause problems down the line, however, if you wind up having a fight with your DP. If you buy a camera of your own, the DP can't just pack up all of his shit and go home when he finds out you have been screwing his girlfriend, leaving you perfectly fucked.

Light kit

Unless you're shooting your entire film outside in the sunlight, you need to have a light kit.[9] You can go hit up your local camera shop or cruise Internet auction sites* for good deals. When it comes to the basic set up, you will at least need to have a key light, a fill light, and a back light. You can then use diffusion and filters to create whatever mood you're going for. Those bowl-like clamp lights you pick up at Home Depot work fine, as do worklights. Worklights have the added benefit of coming on stands of their own, but they are retardedly** bright and should be deflected and diffused when used on set. Also, be sure to get room temperature bulbs. You'll also need spare bulbs, dimmer switches, and a power strip or two. If you run an Internet search for the phrase "DIY light kit" you can find plans for creating your own light kit on the cheap. There is no point in making a movie if nobody can see the damn thing.

Boom mic with windshield

Nothing, and I mean nothing, ruins a movie like shitty sound. In fact, bad sound is often the dead giveaway of a low-budget movie.

---

[8]I use a 35mm cameraman with a nice package as well as a nice camera package.

[9]Young, first-time digital filmmakers often make the mistake of thinking they can shoot their movie with no lights.

*LONELY FOOTNOTE GUY SAYS ... I'm cruising some Internet sites now, but it's not really helping. I wish I had a friend. It's kind of sad being shoved down at the bottom of the page like this.

**EDITOR'S NOTE: Okay, seriously, Lloyd ... Can we tone down the use of the word "retard" or any variation of the word "retard" just a little bit? Just a little?

To avoid this unfortunate distinction, you should invest in a high-quality microphone and windscreen. Unless, of course, you actually want your actors to sound like they are talking with a mouthful of marbles.* Before shooting, you may want to take the time to learn how to properly mic a shot without having the boom shadow run across your actor's face or letting the microphone drift into frame.

Grip kit

Ah, the hardship-filled existence of the lowly grip. These are the guys who have to carry all the shit around and set it all up for you.** You get to yell at them a lot. A solid grip kit includes Gaffers tape, leather work gloves, wooden clothespins, scissors, cable ties, measuring tape, thick black markers, a utility tool, extension cords, and whatever else you think you might have to keep handy while in production. Another great tool to use on your low-budget, independent movie is a wheelchair and ply wood. This can be used as a makeshift dolly or to wheel yourself around after your crew beats you up.[10]

Tripod

You probably don't want your film to look like it was shot by a blind midget being blown up by a Taliban terrorist, so you need to invest in a good tripod. Cheaper tripods will wobble, fucking up your otherwise brilliant shots. If it comes down to feeding your actors or buying a good tripod, have somebody haggle some day-old bagels from the local coffee shop for your actors and spend the dough on a tripod. But, don't get glued to your tripod! If you watch my films,[11] you will see that I use a lot of handheld shots.

---

*EDITOR'S NOTE: I'm pretty sure that you wanted to say a mouthful of something else here, but I appreciate that you didn't.

**A NOTE FROM YOUR FRIENDLY FOOTNOTE GUY: Boy, do I understand that! I think I've mentioned that footnoting is one of the least appreciated professions in the publishing world. I don't even know if the editor checks these things.

[10]The Wheelchair dolly and plywood was used on *The Battle of Love's Return*.

[11]Several members of the Troma Team suggested I make a joke here about how no one would ever want to watch my films. But I'm not going to do it.

Tape stock

I suggest purchasing only the highest quality DV tape for your production, and sticking to that particular brand only. You see, different companies use different methods of lubricating their video tape. If you start using different brands of tape, you can cause a serious build-up of residue in your camera. This will result in all of your hard work getting chewed up when you try to play it back or rewind it.

Prior to shooting, make sure your tape has been properly time stamped (a process known as "blacking out"). When you finally transfer your award-winning footage to your computer, it will be extremely important that your tape has been time stamped. Most editing programs read the time stamp in a linear manner. If you don't black out the tape, every time you remove the tape from the camera or shut it off, a new time stamp is created when you start to shoot again. Your software will get confused over which time stamp to follow when you're capturing the footage. If you have time stamped the entire tape, the camera won't re-write the time stamp every time you turn the camera off or remove the tape repeatedly.

To black out a tape, put the DV tape in the camera, leave the lens on, and disable the microphone. Hit the record button and let the camcorder roll until the tape has recorded 60 minutes of complete black and silence. Rewind the tape and mark it so that you know you have time stamped this tape. This may sound like a pain in the ass, but it will help you avoid heartache and frustration later on down the line.

Now, if you can't afford all of the equipment listed above, don't sweat it. The important thing is to set the wheels into motion and start getting your movie made. Equipment can always be borrowed, stolen, or purchased from a store with an extremely lenient return policy and then taken back for a full refund. Just be sure to scrape off the fake blood and jism from the boom pole before you try to take it back. At worst, you can put together your equipment piecemeal as more funds become available. Giving someone a role in your film who just so happens to have a little extra cash or equipment of their own is a nice way to bump up that production value. Who knows, the next Ron Jeremy might just be discovered in your movie!

ANOTHER NOTE FROM MY EDITRIX

---------------------------Original Message---------------------------

From: elinor@repress.com
Sent: June 1, 2008 10:13 AM
To: Lloyd Kaufman <lloyd@troma.com >
Subject: chapters you sent
Dear Lloyd,

Coming along very well, Lloyd. This chapter had some good information for
first-time filmmakers. I'm still a little concerned that we aren't focused too much
on the directing aspect, however. I mean, talking about the advantages of a
writing partner is good. Maybe that would be better reserved for a book about
screenwriting? I'm not sure . . . Think about it.

Also, there are several libel issues that we should discuss. These definitely need to
be taken out before publication.

Best,
Elinor

Sent via BlackBerry by AT&T
---------------------------End Message---------------------------

PRACTICAL DIRECTING TIPS, AS PER ELINOR "HOW TO LOOK LIKE A DIRECTOR"

I am often asked what it is that qualifies one to actually be a director. The
question is often phrased as, "Who the hell do you think you are?" or "What
gives you the right?" These are great questions, and I would like to answer
them here. It's quite simple, actually. I LOOK like a director. Here are a few
tips to help you look like a director TOO!

1. Be the best dressed person on the set. This will automatically give you an
   air of authority, and your crew will instinctively respect you.

2. Be the worst dressed person on the set. This shows your crew that you
   don't care about politics or pleasing the man. You are just there to make
   some fucking art and do your thing. They will instinctively respect you.

3. Hold your hands up in front of your face to create a small box-like shape with your fingers. Then peer through the finger box like you are envisioning the next shot. This serves no real function, but it makes you look really cool.

4. Scowl. Scowl like you mean it. Directing is the hardest job in the movie business, and you need to let everyone know it. That way they can respect you. When you see a PA walk by carrying a 60-lb camera case, scowl at her. She won't be able to help feeling sorry for you and all the hard work you do.

5. Wear an awesome hat. Something really fucking pretentious. Everyone will love you for it. Just don't tell anyone where you got the awesome hat, because then they might want to wear one like it, and then everyone will look like a director.

6. Wear a director's viewfinder around your neck. This is the true sign of a real director. Just look at the picture of me on the cover of this book. You could tell I was the director right away, couldn't you!

LLOYD'S INTERVIEW WITH HIS GOOD PAL, STAN LEE

In case this is the first book you've ever read and have no idea who Stan Lee is, he is the founder of Marvel Comics and the co-creator and writer of Spider Man, X-Men, The Incredible Hulk, Daredevil, Iron Man, *and many other iconic characters and comics.*

Aside from being a comic book hero, Stan has also had his fair share of work in the film industry. After all, who could forget his spectacular narration on Troma's very own Citizen Toxie!

Lloyd: You've worked with the great, great directors, with mediocre directors, and the maybe not so good directors. Could you talk a bit about what you see as the principles of film directing?

Stan: Well, you do know I'm no great authority on directing, but I've been lucky because most of the people who've done Marvel movies have been great directors and, well, I wasn't always on the set. I was only on the set for a few hours doing my cameo in each movie. What I've found is that the one thing they had in common was the great relationship they had with the actors, as well as a great way of expressing themselves in order to help the actor really understand the essence of the scene. Then they have the ability, after they've explained it and have confidence in their cast and crew, to get out of the way

FIGURE 3.5 Lloyd Kaufman and Stan Lee on the set of the original 1938 Saturday Night Fever.

and let it just happen normally and naturally. I have never been with a good director who lost his temper or shouted or screamed at people or did any of the things they let directors do in movie comedies, or films where they show how temperamental directors are. As a matter of fact, they don't even dress funny. One director that always impressed me was Sam Raimi who did *Spiderman*. He's the only director who actually wears a suit and tie to work. The rest of the crew looks like commandos in field jackets and jeans and so forth. Sam looks like a visitor from the city. I asked him once . . . I said "how come you always wear a suit?" and he said his father taught him "when you work with people, always show them respect," which was an unusual thing to hear. I think Sam is really great but, as I said, of all the directors I've been lucky enough to work with, it's Jon Favreau.

Lloyd: What did Favreau do?

Stan: He did *Iron Man*. It was a happy set. He has a great sense of humor. He was kidding with the actors, giving them a lot of freedom. Bryan Singer as well; beautiful working with him. He was always so prepared. He knew what he wanted, explained it, and did it. They remind me of you, Lloyd.

Lloyd: Very funny.

Stan: It's true.

Lloyd: Do these guys have storyboards? Did you manage to see if they have shot lists?

Stan: Well they always have a clipboard with a million papers on it. To be honest I've never seen it. I know a lot of them do storyboards for a lot of scenes of course, and they have a lot of notes. If they don't have notes, their assistants are always walking, loaded with papers.

Lloyd: If you were young, let's say a film school graduate, or just a fanatic, and you wanted to get into the mainstream . . . do you have any suggestions?

Stan: The only thing that I've heard is that most directors come out of film school and get a job working for a movie company or some sort of production company. They start out as an assistant's-assistant's-assistant and work their way up. But some actually direct a movie in film school and it looks good and people notice it and then they take it to one of the film festivals — the Sundance Film Festival — and, if they're lucky, somebody notices it. Didn't George Lucas get started by producing something like *THX 1138* in film school and people were impressed? I'll be honest with you, when I was young; I wish I had gone to film school. I would have loved to learn how to produce and make a movie. I don't know if I wanted to be a director because . . . I'd love to be a director, if only it didn't take up so much time. When they do a big film, they can be away from home for two or three or four months. It's being on the set everyday and the thing that amazes me is that directors can keep their interests up whilst they're involved in all the little details like: "let's do this scene over because the light wasn't right, or let's do that over because the sound quality wasn't right." You do one scene over and over and then you'll have to wait for maybe a few hours because the camera needs to be set up for the next scene, which you'll do over and over. I don't think I've got the temperament. And you know better than anyone that a certain temperament is needed for that sort of thing.

Lloyd: Have you noticed certain directors along the way that make mistakes?

Stan: Well, the early *Captain America* movie wasn't that good. Real low-budget movie. I don't know what specific mistakes were made, but it looked like a low-budget movie. There was *Sgt. Fury*, which had gone on television as a movie of the week or something and everything about it I thought was pretty good. David Hasselhoff played Sgt. Fury, but the mistake they made there, I think, is the girl they cast as the villain. She was a good actress, but wasn't right for that role. And for me it ruined the whole thing. Every so often if you have the wrong person in a major role, or the wrong music, or the wrong approach or attitude . . . There are so many elements that all have to come together and gel perfectly. I feel funny telling this to you. You're a director.

Lloyd: Have you seen cases where people have compromised? Maybe they've tried to re-invent a script to fit television, or a market, and that ruined the film?

Stan: Very often when something is intended for television, they feel the need to change the original script to have it more accommodating for the TV screen. Very often that ruins it, but that happens with movies too. Often you'll have a successful novel that people enjoyed as a book and yet, when they film it, unfortunately they will leave out the very element that made the book a success. Sometimes that element is magnificent dialogue, but most directors don't want their movies to consist of "talking heads" as they call it, so they'll leave out the dialogue which fascinated the readers the most. There could be countless other things that are left behind. Sometimes a book could sell well because, even though it was a serious story, there was an underlying tone of humor which gave it a good balance, and the director either has no sense of humor or didn't feel the humor belonged in the movie. From what I've seen, the director really *is* in charge. Even when the producers are on the set he's the one who determines the mood of the movie. He determines what the pace is. He determines what to emphasize, what to minimize. I mean it's really in the hands of the director. Even when the script is written, the director still can let it go in many directions.

Lloyd: Do you recall any specifics about books or movies? To me *Daredevil* was good because . . .

Stan: *Daredevil*. I'm probably one of the only people that I've spoken to — I speak to myself often — who thinks . . . who was the fellow that played Daredevil?

Lloyd: Ben Affleck

Stan: Anyway, I thought it was good, but I thought that there was too much suffering in *Daredevil*. Originally *Daredevil* was of a lighter tone and I felt somehow there were too many scenes that were too dark. We didn't need that business in the church at the beginning and end, but I believe that there were some beautifully done things in the *Daredevil* movie.

So many of the really successful directors have their own style. You can recognize their hand in whatever it is that they do. Quentin Tarantino — you can almost always tell right away that it's one of his movies. You have that same thing; you can always recognize a Troma movie directed by Lloyd Kaufman. And that's great. People spend a lifetime trying to get their own stamp of individuality, and you can always tell a Troma movie directed by Lloyd Kaufman. The unfortunate thing about it is that it's catered to a certain audience and they have a lot of sex and violence, and it's all humorous, but it's still there. That makes it hard to get enough screen time and a lot of theater seats. You can't get into enough theaters. And, maybe this is bad advice, but I think the day should come when you do a movie like *Sgt. Kabukiman*, and you do it like it's a comedy for a general audience. Not an R-rating, but a G-rating. So many of your movies have a clever concept, they're always parodying something. Like *Toxic Avenger* — it's a great idea. A superman who is that ugly and he has a mop and a pail — it's funny! But because of all the violence and all the far-out stuff, you can't get it played for the general audience. So I think it would be great if sometime in the future . . . for your next . . . even your *Tromeo & Juliet* here, everything is a parody of something. Well I think the next time you want to do a parody of something, you ought to write it, but leave out the things that will make it not acceptable to most theaters, but still make sure that you have your own far-out humor in there. If that's possible without the other element then, I think, the sky would be the limit. Your basic concepts are great! You're a great director, but you direct movies that only a certain young audience will go for. And that's not bad — you've got your own niche — and you've got something most people don't have, you've got your own personal recognizable style. As your friend and fan, I just wish that that style would be more distributed around the field.

Now take something like *Sgt. Kabukiman*, so many things enter into what makes it a success. Say you have someone like Jim Carey playing the role and let's say you eliminated some things that were too far out. You'd have a great actor, a great comic, a great concept, and you might have a film that could be another *Bruce Almighty*. To me, something like *Bruce Almighty* would be your type of story, but it didn't have any of the objectionable stuff in it. So they were able to just go with the funny stuff. All of your main concepts and your plots are funny, but you don't have enough confidence in your funny stuff and you put in all the other things. Which I'll admit, your fans love, but it doesn't get you into enough theaters.

So, if you were to decide to come up with an off-the-wall concept, as you always do with some sort of parody, and you'd say to yourself, "I'm going to see if I can get an Adam Sandler, Jim Carey, or Ben Stiller," you know somebody like that for the role, and instead of spending a million dollars or so and doing it in a studio in NY, come out to LA and spend 5 million dollars. I'll borrow it from friends — only joking. Maybe we'll spend a few million and for once I'll go for a mainstream wild comedy, because they do well! Things like the *Wedding Crashers* and *Knocked Up*. Those are your type of movies, but they're done in a family way! But I feel silly telling this to you, because you're a successful director and I would like to see you more recognized.

Chapter four

Preproduction: My Own Private Idaho (and by Idaho, I, of course, mean Hell)

It's 11 a.m. and I'm sitting in the new office that Michael Herz and I share in the Troma Building. Michael's wife Maris has insisted that, unlike our old building, this new Tromaville headquarters is going to actually look somewhat like an office, as opposed to a seedy den of sin or the bedroom of a sexually repressed teenage boy.[1] As such, she has had the interns spend two days scraping 30 years worth of stickers off the filing cabinets and has, so far, forbidden anyone to touch the freshly painted white walls, much less hang the Troma posters that covered the urine-soaked walls of the old building. In her quest for cleanliness, she has also, for some reason, refused to hang window shades of any kind. Maybe she's afraid I'll urinate on them like a cat or something. It's almost noon and the

---

[1]Which is how the slum we previously occupied for 30 years looked.

sun is gunning for me. Scattered in front of me, though I can barely see it for the glare, is a haphazard pile of wood and screws, which, in a perfect world, would be a bookcase. Out the bare and unnaturally clean window, a group of preschool children from the Catholic daycare across the street are banging tambourines and ringing bells. I decide to put off the bookshelf assembly for another minute and get up to look out the window. The Pope is in town, and the kids and their teachers are putting on a parade. It's adorable. It's heartwarming. It's also really fucking loud, and I'm tempted to open the window and tell them to shut their little faces. Fortunately, the bare and unnaturally clean windows don't open. I pull a Troma 35th anniversary poster out from one of the many boxes around my desk, and tape it to the window. With one simple act, I have managed to best the sun, the Pope, and above all, Maris. Time to get back to work. It is me versus this bookshelf. Michael has been on my case for the last two weeks to either finish it or get the pile of wood out of the office we share. Up until now I have been successful in my procrastination. After all, Troma is in the middle of promoting its newest film, *Poultrygeist: Night of the Chicken Dead*. There are interviews to be done, festivals to attend, theater owners to fellate. And Michael[2] sure isn't going to do it.

But today is different. Fueled by two cups of coffee and foolish ambition, I have busted out my pathetic excuse for a toolbox[3] and decided to make a go of it. Unfortunately, things are not going as I had hoped.

"Son of a bitch!" I mutter to myself. I down another gulp of coffee and attach one piece of wood to a bigger piece of wood. After one particularly difficult turn of a screw, I realize that I have successfully secured one of the shelves to the brand new carpet. Michael is going to love this. Scratch that — Maris is going to love it even more. I'm losing this battle against an inanimate object. I'm unfocused; my movements are haphazard and sloppy. It's almost like I'm having sex.[4]

---

[2]The Michael I keep referring to is my partner of 35 years, Michael Herz. He is handsome, muscular, brilliant, and absolutely hates appearing in public or in the media. He may be a cyborg.

[3]Not to be confused with James Gunn's nickname for my penis, "pathetic excuse for a tool."

[4]This is true. Though it's usually more expensive and less time consuming than this shitty bookcase.

Just as I insert the last screw, Michael walks in, fresh from the gym, with his daily wonton soup. I sit back proudly and admire my handiwork, fully expecting him to do the same. In the process, however, I also manage to knock my cup of coffee onto the new carpet.

"Son of a bitch ..." I grumble again.

"Son of a bitch ..." says Michael. "Maris is gonna fucking kill you."

The bookcase in front of me is a sad old Jew's equivalent of Charlie Brown's Christmas tree. Beside me, coffee has spread itself out on the carpet like a dark pool of blood. It looks remarkably like the blood in Michael's eyes. I start to mention that resemblance to him, then think better of it. Also, Maris[5] may, in fact, actually kill me. I look back at the bookcase and then back at the coffee stain. Neither of these are battles that I'm going to win this morning. At least the bookcase won't need to be steam cleaned, so I decide to focus on that. I look again at the picture on the box and, as my frustration swells, I'm about two seconds away from crying like a little girl.

"How in the hell did you manage to fuck it up like that?" Michael asks. That's when it hits me. Putting together this wooden abomination was exactly like doing preproduction on a film. I had rushed into this too soon. I was sloppy, unprepared, and I had ended up with proverbial blood on the floor. If only I had carefully prepared for this task, assembled the proper tools, and organized all of the parts beforehand, I would have built a perfect bookcase in a fraction of the time it had taken me to cobble together this abstract piece of art.[6]

THE POINT?

That's what preproduction is all about. It's the time in which you carefully chart your course. A piss-poor preproduction will result in a piss-poor film. It all makes perfect sense.

Elated, I pick the soggy cup up off the floor and inform my scowling partner that the bookcase will have to wait. I have some

---

[5]The Maris that I keep referring to is Michael's attractive and young-looking wife, who also runs our office. I fear her, and she knows it.

[6]Well, that's not entirely true. The bookcase still probably would have looked like a piece of shit. But at least it would have been a piece of shit I was proud of.

writing to do. Also, there is a big black stain on the carpet that someone will need to clean up.

THIS MAY HURT A LITTLE

The time has finally arrived! After enduring countless sleepless, sex-deprived nights, you now hold in your grubby little mitts a script that you are pretty satisfied with. Stand up, take a bow, and pat yourself on the back! Finished? Good. Now sit the fuck down and listen. Your script is going to change, so deal with it. The hard part is about to begin. It's preproduction time, Lil' Mama.*

A lot of people think that preproduction is the time when you cast your film and decide upon a shooting schedule. Well, those people are right, but there's a lot more to it. In an earlier draft of this chapter, I called preproduction the calm before the storm. Well, that's a load of bullshit. Preproduction is the storm before the storm. It's the hail before the blizzard. It's my least favorite part of filmmaking, and often leaves me in a semi-vegetative state of depression. But don't let that get you down! Think of this stage as a pre-emptive strike against the shit storm. It's when you will meticulously assemble your battle plan before charging into the war of movie making. Use this time wisely, because the better prepared you are, the better your shoot will be.

A GLIMPSE INSIDE LLOYD'S HEAD

A few days into preproduction of Troma's latest film, *Poultrygeist*, I panicked. Now, because I like to maintain a certain air of intelligence, I double-checked the spelling of "panicked" before I wrote it down here, because I couldn't for the life of me remember if it had a "k" in it or not. It does, but here's what else I found:

> Panic — a sudden overwhelming fear, with or without cause, that produces hysterical or irrational behavior, and that often spreads quickly through a group of persons or animals.

Yeah, that's about right. This animal was running scared. Things weren't going according to plan. Not that we had a plan, but that's what preproduction is for, right? Theoretically, yes, but try formulating a plan that incorporates

---

*A NOTE FROM YOUR FRIENDLY FOOTNOTE GUY: I have to admit that I was a little disappointed with the footnotes in the last couple of chapters. But I feel like we're back on track. That James Gunn joke was hilarious!

musical numbers; chicken feathers; an abandoned, leaky, fire-trap of a McDonald's; and explosive diarrhea. Lots of explosive diarrhea. Luckily, I approached the preproduction problem in the same calm and level-headed manner in which I approach all Troma problems. I grabbed a bottle of Popov Vodka, crawled under Michael's desk, and tried to rock myself to sleep.[7] Just as I started to reach an almost trance-like state, I swear to god the Toxic Avenger himself appeared in front of me. This is new, I thought to myself, but somehow oddly exciting. Maybe it was just a Troma employee in a Toxie mask trying to mess with my head, but either way . . . The next several minutes went something like this:

FIGURE 4.1 Lloyd Kaufman, about to demonstrate how he earned the Fluffer Society Lifetime Achievement Award.

---

[7]The carpet beneath Michael's desk is relatively sanitary, as he spends most of the time with his feet up on the desk. Contrast this with the carpet under my desk, which is marked with permanent knee impressions.

TOXIE: What's wrong Lloyd? You look a little upset.

ME: Oh boy, Toxie, you have no idea. We're making this movie about chicken Indian zombies and you know how much I hate preproduction. And I didn't even tell you yet that it's a musical. A musical! And we don't even have any songs written.

TOXIE: That sounds tough, Lloyd. But haven't you done this before?

ME: I've done it about 30 times, but each time only seems to get worse, not better. It's like I'm in one of those machines.

TOXIE: What machines?

ME: You know, the ones where you're strapped in and you're in, like, a tunnel and you can't move and you can't see anything.

TOXIE: I have no idea what you're talking about.

ME: It doesn't matter. My point is that I've got about six months, worth of planning and scheduling to do and only about six days to do it. The people around me all hate me and/or are idiots and I can't threaten them with anything because I'm not paying them and I'm already making them sleep on the floor and withholding food. I want to make a great movie, but the shit just keeps piling up. Everywhere around me is just shit, shit, shit. What do I do, Toxie?

(*Right around this time, my Toxie image begins to get a little fuzzy and he just stares at me with his droopy eye as he fades away.*)

TOXIE: Did you mean an MRI machine, Lloyd?

ME: Yeah, that's it. An MRI machine . . .

And then he's gone, and I'm alone under the desk, strangely, with an erection. Something had to change, and I was going to have to be the one to change it. Toxie was right. I've done this preproduction thing countless times before. I'm a fucking director, for goodness sake. It was time to man up. And that's when the answer hit me. Get out from under Michael's desk, finish the bottle of Popov, and fire Andy Deemer.

-------------------------Original Message-------------------------
From: elinor@repress.com
Sent: June 22, 2008 10:14AM
To: Lloyd Kaufman <lloyd@troma.com >
Subject: Andy Deemer?

Hey Lloyd,

Just a quick note- glanced over the last chapter and I'm wondering who Andy
Deemer is. I don't think you've mentioned him in previous chapters. This might
confuse people.

Best,
Elinor

Sent via BlackBerry by AT&T
-------------------------End Message-------------------------

-------------------------Original Message-------------------------
From: Lloyd Kaufman <lloyd@troma.com >
Sent: June 22, 2008 12:31PM
To: Elinor <elinor@repress.com >
Subject: RE: Andy Deemer?

Don't worry Elinor. This will all make sense in the next 30 pages or so.

xoxo

the fourth Jonas brother
-------------------------End Message-------------------------

AN ARMY OF ONE* . . . RARELY WINS THE WAR

By preparing yourself properly, you will be able to foresee any problems
that may arise during production, nipping them in the foreskin before
they rear their ugly penis monster heads. At the very least you should
have a few plans in place just in case these problems occur. (They

*SOLITARY FOOTNOTE GUY SAYS: You know, one is also the loneliest number. Please
call me at 718-391-0110 and ask for Pedro le Petit. Someone . . . Anyone . . .

will, without a doubt, occur. So you might as well plan how you're going to deal with them now.) How are you going to feed everyone? Where are people going to sleep? Who will remain in the production office while everyone else is on set? Who will make sure that everyone has directions to all of the locations? These are just a few of the issues you are going to have to address during preproduction. But you can't do it all by yourself. You're going to need some help. It's time to put together your team. I get very involved with choosing the staff. Everyone must be 100% devoted to my vision — even the kid who arranges the lunches or cleans the bathrooms (which sometimes seem interchangeable on a Troma set). I can't stress the following point strongly enough: The absolute most important aspect of your production team is that they must be 100% DEDICATED TO THE PROJECT! The people you handpick to help you make your film can't be in it for money, but rather for what they will gain from the experience of working on a feature film. They should be motivated by the opportunity to contribute to the project and take on responsibilities they would not otherwise be given on a conventional film.*

THE DREAM . . . ER . . . TROMA TEAM

Assembling your team is easily one of the most important aspects of the entire filmmaking process. You want your production staff and crew to work like a well-oiled machine,[8] a single creative organism with only one goal in mind: to get your movie made the way that you want to make it. The ideal production team will quickly bond as a family, pulling together during even the most trying times to make the impossible happen. Unfortunately, the family that most production teams resemble tends to be the inbred, infighting group of freaks from *The Texas Chainsaw Massacre*. You can't allow this to happen, or your film will turn to shit quicker than you can say, "Oh shit, my precious movie is turning to shit!"

I'm often quoted as saying that we at Troma don't take ourselves seriously, but we do take our movies extremely seriously. This is not bullshit. Sure, one might assume by looking at *Poultrygeist* that

---

*DESPERATE FOOTNOTE GUY SAYS . . . I have a no-interest mortgage and I need some cash fast. THIS SPACE FOR RENT!! THIS SPACE FOR RENT!! THIS SPACE FOR RENT!!

[8]I like my hairless male PAs to be particularly well-oiled.

we are a carefree, drug-riddled cacophony of chaos and naked boobies. But that's only after we have taken care of business. The film has to be the most important aspect of your crew's lives for as long as they are involved in it. Not getting laid. Not getting drunk. As the director, you are the captain of your own ship, and you need to make sure that your team understands this fact well in advance. Anyone who is slightly negative must be shown the door.[9]

YOU SAY HYPOCRITE LIKE IT'S A BAD THING

As unpopular as this may sound, I usually find it best to be wary of people who are married[10] or who have children. In fact, I suggest you avoid these people like the clap. Yeah, I know, I'm an asshole. The fact is, I'm married and have kids, but the film has always been top priority in our family life. I grill prospective production staff who are married very vigorously and try to persuade them not to work on my film. Nothing can bring a production to a screeching halt like someone who has to suddenly leave your location in Buffalo to take care of some inane family situation. Since your crew is most likely working for little or no money, it can be a gigantic pain in the ass to convince this someone that he should remain on his $100/week job securing parking places for your trucks in Manhattan while his wife is having a miscarriage in Hoboken.

THE LAST LINE SUMS IT UP HERE

When it comes to your core crew, I find it best to take on those fresh, eager-to-please individuals who have no idea of what is impossible. You need people who are energetic and don't know the meaning of the word "impossible"; people who can figure out how to get miracles done with hardly any resources at their disposal — not a bunch of know-it-all pricks who constantly moan about how things can't be accomplished. The amazing Kiel Walker graduated from college[11] in 2004 and by the summer of 2005 he was working as a producer on *Poultrygeist*. Prior to this, Kiel had never been on a

---

[9]Even those who stay must often be shown the door so that they can distinguish it from the window or from a goat. When you ask your PA for the script changes and they bring you a goat, you know you're in trouble.

[10]This also applies to people who are regularly shacking up.

[11]Yale University, in fact, and he still ended up working for Troma . . . Hahahaha!

movie set, yet he managed the $500,000 budget, fired unpaid actors and staff, and jumped head first into both the bloody meat grinder and a giant "General Chicken" suit.

Likewise, Troma Producer Andy Deemer[12] also had no on-set[13] filmmaking experience, yet he came through for us on *Poultrygeist*. Aside from being in charge of our $500,000 budget, it was Andy's responsibility, among others, to handle over 300 actor persons (you may know them as "extras") at a time. Keep in mind that these fine folks were asked to work for weeks at a time with no pay, all so they could bake in the scorching summer heat day after day as protesters outside of the American Chicken Bunker, our evil corporate fast food chain in the film. Not only that, but we needed all of those same actor persons to return some time later as transformed chicken Indian zombies with beaks and feathers glued on and be filmed all night long for no pay or food whatsoever. Andy smothered all his responsibilities and made miracles happen when we needed him to. He didn't know that we had given him an impossible task. Both Walker and Deemer approached their jobs with none of the bullshit baggage acquired from years of working in the film industry. These are exactly the kind of people you need on your crew. They also both got copious amounts of ass.[14]

ONE OF MANY WAYS TO AVOID INFECTION ON A TROMA SET

It's during this period that the cream will begin to rise to the top, and you will get a better idea as to which team members are staff stars and which ones are staff infections. That way you can cherry-pick the most talented and dedicated production assistants (PA) from the production staff and place them strategically in different departments of the crew. A lot of what I've been talking about sounds like producer stuff, but as director, you should make it your stuff. It will help you.

---

[12]You may remember that I mentioned Andy before. The fact is, I did fire him. Several times. It was actually Michael Herz's wife Maris who convinced me that I was being a complete idiot by getting rid of someone like Andy. Thanks Maris.

[13]Andy had worked in preproduction on *Tromeo & Juliet* and had actually written one of the early drafts of the scripts, which I rejected. I had to get him drunk in Nashville to convince him to come back to Troma. Ha!

[14]Mostly mine.

FIGURE 4.2 *The 2008 Republican National Convention.*

THE FILM CREW

After assembling your production team, it's time to put together your actual film crew. These are the fine folks that will wade through a sea of heartbreak and shit with you every step of the shoot. Choose these people wisely, otherwise you'll find yourself sad and alone in your most desperate hour.

Emma Brown came to Buffalo, New York, from London to volunteer as an unpaid PA on *Poultrygeist*. Ignoring jet lag and the fright and trauma of being driven by me from New York City to Buffalo, so devoted was she to our fowl project that, sleep be damned, she immediately threw herself into cleaning the filthy grease-coated derelict McDonald's location that was to become our American Chicken Bunker fast food restaurant. She also designed and drew some of the wonderful poster-sized ads for "Cluckwork Orange" before even going to sleep.[15]

---

[15] I choose to believe that this was due to her enthusiasm. It may have had something to do with the water boarding as well. I guess we'll never know.

It was obvious to me that Emma would be totally loyal and devoted to *Poultrygeist* so, as a sort of positive force, I inserted her into the camera crew as the "clapper" gyno. The assistant cameraman, Arsineo, eventually inserted himself into Emma and today they are married.

On extremely small productions, each individual on your crew will most likely take on more than one position of responsibility. Here is a short list of individuals you will need on your crew to get your film made. I would suggest that you only actually use one person for each position, but hey — you do what you've got to do.

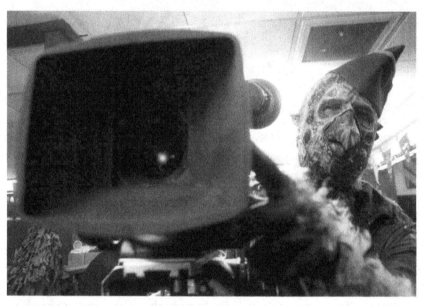

FIGURE 4.3 *Rosie O'Donnell visits the set of Poultrygeist.*

Assistant director (AD)

The single most important thing to remember when choosing an AD is that you need someone who is incredibly driven, capable, and who doesn't have his head stuck firmly up his own ass. Sounds like it should be a breeze, right? The only problem is, anyone who actually has these all-important qualifications probably isn't going to want a job as shitty as unpaid AD.

The AD is the poor bastard who has to deal with all of the people-oriented issues on the set. He has to be the lubricant that helps everyone come together smoothly. If you can, assign someone you know who is a real "people person" to this task. If your AD's idea of conflict resolution is punching someone in the mouth, you may want to reconsider. I made Trent Haaga my AD on *Citizen Toxie: The Toxic Avenger IV*, and the last I heard he was recently released from his second stint in Rikers for stabbing a car wash attendant in the neck with a pencil.*

Director of photography (DP)

This is the person who actually operates the camera. If you think that operating a camera is as easy as pointing it at your actors and hitting a button, I suggest you get someone to do this for you. You'll work more closely with the DP while shooting your movie than with any other person on the set, so if you don't share a common vision with this person you'll be setting yourself up for one hell of a horrendous experience, as each of you will attempt to impose your will on the other until someone either breaks or goes insane. On several films, I have utilized the services of the very talented Brendan Flynt as my DP. Since Brendan knows my working style so well, we're able to get a hell of a lot more work done than I would if I were working with a new DP each time. Where someone else might take all day setting up the lights for that "perfect shot," Brendan knows that I never stop shooting a scene after just one take. Instead, Brendan will get the lights set up in a reasonable manner and then continue to tinker with the set-up in between takes. By the time I'm satisfied with the coverage and performances, Brendan is satisfied with his lighting. Brendan also lets me operate[16] the camera whenever I feel necessary. Most DPs won't permit this. He also works pretty cheap, which is nice.

Script supervisor

Your script supervisor keeps track of what you have already shot, in what order it was shot, and any changes made to the script as you shoot. A good script supervisor will also keep an eye out for any continuity errors. This means that they should know the script inside and out, and maintain clear communication with the director and AD. At Troma, we shoot all of our rehearsals (on video tape,

---

*EDITOR'S NOTE: Not funny, Lloyd, and also not true. Trent Haaga is a great people person and a successful Hollywood screenwriter. He told me so himself.

[16] I'm actually surprised that he still allows this, after that time I misunderstood what he meant by "operate" and accidentally amputated the boom man's leg.

much as it does the actors, and it's the perfect opportunity for your
script supervisor to get a head start on preparing for his job.

Sound person/boom operator

Unless you're planning on filming a silent movie, you're going to
need somebody on set who can record all of the dialogue for you.
This may sound like an easy enough task, but you would be surprised
at how many times I have shot the perfect take, only to find out that
my sound monkey/boom operator forgot to turn the microphone on.

A good boom operator will know when the sound is too hot
(blown out and inaudible), where the microphone should be placed
for optimum sound (near the actor's mouth is usually a good start),
and manage to avoid drifting the boom mic into frame or casting
a shadow over the actors. The boom operator should also be adept
at killing any ambient noise that can seep into your audio, creating problems when it comes time to mix the sound. This includes
electrical hums such as florescent lights and refrigerators, passing
airplanes and car horns, and the whimpering dog you kicked when
he forgot to turn the microphone on the first time.

The most glaring sign of a low-budget production is shitty
sound, so you want to make sure that your boom operator knows
what the hell she is doing. People can forgive bad lighting if the
story is interesting, but nobody is going to sit through a movie they
can't hear. You as director should listen to the sound take as well.

HOW THE TROMA SYSTEM PREPARED ME FOR PRISON

By William Akers

I interned at Troma in 1999, during the run-up to *Citizen Toxie: The Toxic
Avenger IV*, and I learned countless skills that I imagined I'd never use outside of a Troma set. Unfortunately, a sordid stream of events led to my arrest
in 2003 and I am now an inmate within the frighteningly Orwellian machine
that is the Texas Department of Criminal Justice. The last time I saw Lloyd
was during the filming of Barak Epstein's women-in-prison opus, *Prison-A-
Go-Go*, in which Lloyd played an evil prison guard. In that creepy Tromatic
irony, shortly after *Prison-A-Go-Go*, to prison I went-went.

My incarceration regrettably gives ammunition to detractors who insist that Troma movies are made for/by murderers, pederasts, and the criminally insane. I'd like to officially debunk this myth; during my journey through the stinking bowels of the prison system, the number of convicts I've met who are familiar with Troma can be counted on the fingers of one severed hand. I've got a Toxie tattoo on my arm that I use as a beacon for captive Troma fans, but most people mistake it for Sloth from *The Goonies*. It's depressing. Occasionally, someone will point at my arm and cry, "Dat's dat Toxic Crusader!" I feel a special connection with these guys — when they park the beef bus where they see fit, I swear they're extra gentle (though sometimes they do make me wear sunglasses just so they can say, "I always did wanna cornhole me a blind bitch!").*

FIGURE 4.4 William Akers, with camera, in better times. As in, before prison.

My Troma experience was an excellent primer for prison life. On the Troma set, the toilet facilities are either substandard or nonexistent. Stories abound of disgruntled crew members defecating in paper lunch sacks. Where Lloyd poops is a mystery though — there isn't a lunch sack on Earth that could contain him! In prison, when we're locked down and the water has been turned off so we can't flush our drugs or shanks or cell phones, we're often forced to shit in a paper sack and throw it out on the walkway. New prisoners balk at the conditions, but I'm used to it — when several steaming sacks litter the cell block, it smells like the Aroma du Troma, indeed!

---

*This is, of course, a reference to both *The Toxic Avenger* and the poetry of Keats.

Bad craft services and prison food? One and the same, really. Actually, this is an area where Troma might be better than prison — some of our meals here look like they belong in Troma's special effects department. Our hot links sometimes contain fingers from latex gloves; the whereabouts of the actual finger the glove contained is a mystery better left unsolved.

Another Troma/prison parallel is the ability of both to reduce grown men to tears. There's a lot of crying on the cell block, though most of it occurs after lights out, and unfortunately, is punctuated by grunts and wet slapping sounds. At Troma, whether from exhaustion or from being reduced to a quivering mass of emotions by one of Lloyd's diatribes, crying is as much a part of the experience as Bromo-Seltzer, fake blood, and Ultra-Slime™.

You know, it occurs to me now as I write this that prisoners are a great untapped resource for low-budget filmmakers. Prison jobs are either unpaid or pay pennies an hour, so salary is a non-issue. They're used to deplorable living conditions and every manner of verbal and physical abuse. Best of all, they need jobs! And if things don't work out, you can always plant some coke on them and snitch them out to their parole officer. Yep, I envision the Troma Team on Lloyd's next production will be culled entirely from Rikers Island. You're welcome, Lloyd!

THE MANSON FAMILY ON LSD WITH VERY LITTLE MONEY . . . AND THE PRODUCTION MANAGER

You want to fill your crew with people who want to make movies themselves one day. People who are looking down the line at their own creative ambitions and are eager to learn from the experience of helping you make your film. You don't want the guy who is content pushing a dolly for the rest of his life. It's not uncommon for people to start out on a Troma film as a PA and eventually find themselves promoted to producers and ADs when they prove themselves invaluable. A few weeks into production, I often take the most capable PA and make him[17] the production manager. This person will be my shadow. She will assist me in running the show. Everything that I know, she should know. We need to eat, sleep, and breathe as a single entity from this

---

[17]In an effort to promote equality among the sexes, I have used an equal number of "he" and "she" pronouns throughout the book. Feel free to go back and count them up. I think you'll be satisfied.

point on. For all intents and purposes, this person will be my Siamese twin. In the past, I have often had my production mangers bathe with me to develop a strong sense of trust and intimacy.

Your production manager will also help you break down the script and schedule the shoot. Take a few of the other more capable individuals and make them your unit manager, location manager, etc. These are the guys that will keep you on track when everything around you is going to shit. Things will usually start to go to shit right after you yell "action!" on your first day.[18]

By taking the time to put together a loyal and useful production staff and crew, and giving them responsibilities that demonstrate how much you trust them, you create a sense of camaraderie. This is important. When I first started working in film, the cast and crew often couldn't give two fucks about loyalty or the director's vision. They were showing up to collect a paycheck and to glom as much extra petty cash and overtime as they could. On *The Final Countdown* (1979) the only people dedicated to the director's vision were star Kirk Douglas, producer Peter Douglas, and myself. Even the director didn't seem to care about the "director's vision." I think this shows up in the film, making what could have been a tremendous film a mediocre one at best. With a more dedicated director, cast, and crew, it could have been spectacular. One of the luxuries of directing a low-budget film is that you can take the time to assemble the crew that you want, without any interference from hacks, unions, or studios.

OUT OF THE FRYING PAN (HELL) AND INTO THE FIRE (HELL)

Now you are chugging right along toward the next stage of preproduction — the casting of your film. Get ready to watch hours of your neighbors and your neighbors' out of town cousins performing interpretive dances to the theme from *Titanic*.* Grab your bottle of Popov and hold on, captain, because it's going to be a bumpy road.

---

[18]Check out *Poultry In Motion: Truth is Stranger Than Chicken*, the edu-mentary about the last Sheryl Crow tour. You'll see what I'm talking about. Available now from www.troma.com on the 3-disc de-clux edition of *Poultrygeist*. BUY TROMA!

*FOOTNOTE GUY SAYS: I'm listening to the theme from *Titanic* right now! Why won't anyone love me??? Lloyd, if you can hear me, I'm considering ordering a Russian bride. What do you think? Write back soon!

Oh, and if you were wondering how that bookcase turned out, I ended up having one of the interns put it together, and it looks beautiful. It's called delegation, and it can be your friend. What was I thinking, trying to put together a fucking Costco bookshelf? I'm a director!

Directors That Pee Sitting Down: An Interview with Penelope Spheeris and Allison Anders

Lindsey Lemke

I'm going to have to interrupt Lloyd and all of his "blah, blah, blah" penis talk for a solid moment. Don't be like an expanding tampon; leave some room for the flow of ovarian energy. Girls can make movies too, you know.

Actually, it was Lloyd's idea to put some "gynoism"* into the book. He asked me to write on the subject of female film directors

---

*In Tromaville, we reject the term "woman" because it contains the word "man." We reject the word "female" because its root word is "male." We prefer the term Gyno-American to describe those lacking a penis.

and why they are such a rarity in this male-dominated industry. It's a subject I hadn't really put much thought into before, probably because I never viewed film directors or any artists by their gender. When it comes to what they do, to me they're all just people making their art and doing their jobs. In fact, some of the strongest female characters in film were born in the minds of men. Even Troma, the ultimate boys club, has created a few kick-ass gynos in its day. I think some of Troma's biggest title films revolve around the strong female persona more than anyone might notice. The character of Jennifer in *Terror Firmer* is a portrayal of a woman paying her dues in film, struggling with vulnerability, and dealing with personal issues in home and romantic life. Eventually Jennifer ends up acting in the film-within-a-film, directing it, and even defeating her love interest/villain using both psychological rape techniques and a physical ass-kicking. We all know some Jennifers. Most of us women are Jennifers. In *Tromeo & Juliet*, Juliet is the Goddess — she is beauty, grace, and poetry[1] in motion. In the scene where she is naked and locked in the glass box, she is Lilith coming out of

FIGURE BC.1 *Penelope Spheeris has a career so bright, she's gotta wear shades.*

[1]Dear Lindsey, don't forget about Wendy in *Poultrygeist*, who is complete "poultry" in motion! xoxo, LK

the seashell. Juliet also is responsible for saving herself in the film, which I love. And last, but not least, Toxie's blind wife Sarah in *Citizen Toxie: The Toxic Avenger IV*. She is all personality wrapped up in the classic blonde bombshell. I can relate! Despite how flighty and naive this character seems due to her condition — and again, I can relate — Sarah is all heart. She is the mother and the caregiver.

I'd hate to say I enjoy some cinema because I relate to its "femininity," but perhaps it's true. We can analyze it all the way down to its sexuality, but I think it goes far beyond just that. But what does it have to do with the people creating it? Even so, I guess we can't help but admit to ourselves that we do see less of the "female persuasion" in many industries including film, politics, pro sports, construction, etc.

Thanks to the Internet, I did some quick research on the subject of female film directors being a rarity and of the film industry being male-dominated. And by quick, I really do mean quick. Lloyd isn't paying me for this chapter, and I actually do have a real job. But on the subject of female directors, surprisingly, there wasn't much info. One article gave insight from women that had actually worked on the sets. One actress mentioned how alienated a woman can feel around a male-dominated cast and director, thus making it hard for a woman to relax and express herself. While this quote may be valid, I personally don't know any women who tense up around men in particular. I personally only tense up when I know I'm surrounded by dicks — and I don't mean that literally. Girls can be dicks too. In another article, a woman mentioned speaking to classrooms of little girls, convincing all but one girl in the class that they wanted to become film directors. That's just weird. That's the same as a plumber lecturing a class of little kids and convincing everyone to be a plumber too. Shit, I remember when I was a kid, I imitated martial arts and fight scenes from TV so I could be Charles Bronson's cinema sidekick protégé. The week before that, I wanted to be a mermaid. . . . Get my drift?

Perhaps it was the long clusters of quotes in these articles that made them seem more exaggerated and preachy. There was so much disgust coming from the women interviewed that by the end, I was a little disgusted too, but at the women themselves. Separating female directors from male directors isn't a feminist thing. It's a separatist thing. The interesting thing about growing up in the early 1990s, as I did, was that we were taught that women can be anything they want. Anything. It was okay for a woman to become an astronaut, just as much as it was okay for her to become a whore. As long as that's what she wanted. Welcome to Generation X!

One of my interview subjects, Penelope Spheeris, once declined a cover of *Vanity Fair* because it focused specifically on female directors. She told them flat out, "I'll do it when you do a cover on male directors." Rock on! But what else would I expect from a director known as a "Rock n' Roll Anthropologist" for her films such as *Suburbia* and *The Decline of Western Civilization*. Oh yeah, and *Wayne's World*. I also interviewed Allison Anders, known for *Gas, Food, Lodging* and *Sugar Town*. She has also directed four *Sex and the City* episodes and is the founder of the Don't Knock the Rock Music & Film Festival. And in case you're wondering . . . Yes, the festival rocks!

I should also add that I didn't interview these two women together. But because this is Lloyd's book and he wanted all the room he could get for the "penis talk," it looks like I interviewed them together. Oh well. You're welcome Lloyd!

A FIRESIDE CHAT WITH PENELOPE SPHEERIS AND ALLISON ANDERS

There seem to be very few female film directors. Why do you think this is? Are women just not interested in directing? Is it the challenges involved to achieving success, or maybe because the industry is too male-dominated, therefore making it too hard to push through the door of the industry due to gender?

PS: For me the problem in the beginning was that I just didn't think I COULD become a director. All directors were guys, so it never occurred to me that I would be allowed to do it until I was well out of film school — after I had my own music video company — after I had produced shorts for *Saturday Night Live* and after I produced my first studio feature *Real Life* in 1978. Here's how I used to describe the landscape back then: A fort guarded by armed soldiers, all male of course, and they wouldn't let anybody in. We always called it The Boys Club. Whenever there are high stakes with money, fame, or any ego-driven goals, the men do whatever they can to keep women out.

AA: There may be more men and boys who want to direct, but I don't think women are not interested or that it's too difficult to take on. There is no job on earth women haven't taken on, so I don't think movie directing would daunt them any more than running a country, say.

FIGURE BC.2 Allison Anders, in the midst of taking charge.

I read an article that discussed why female film directors are such a rarity. It mentioned one of the major reasons being the moving of heavy equipment, as well as handling and directing a crew of 100–150 large men carrying that equipment. It's much like giving orders to an army unit. What are your thoughts on this statement?

AA: Directing requires none of that. Even on the lowest budget set you can ask for a chair. Even if you're in the middle of nowhere, someone is there with, at the very least, an apple box to set under your ass to sit on! Male directors don't carry that stuff around. Are you kidding? Director's chairs were one of the first inventions in the biz! AND even if the job did require heavy lifting, there are plenty of female grips and electricians now who put that argument to rest.

PS: I was in film school at UCLA in the late 1960s, early 1970s. Film students checked the equipment out of a place called the tech office. I was the first woman who was ever allowed to work in the tech office because they thought women could not pick up the heavy equipment. What the staff did not know is that I was actually pregnant while working there and I worked through the eighth month of pregnancy picking up heavy equipment. So those who are saying that women can't physically do it are just grasping at straws, trying to come up with more reasons to keep women out of The Boys Club. I pick up heavy equipment all the time on the set because I like to help out and it's good exercise when you're stuck in a director's chair for 12 hours a day. I can't tell you how many times a grip or a gaffer jokingly said they were going to report me to the union.

Have you ever felt that your gender was an issue during your years of filmmaking?

PS: I am a contemporary of Scorsese, De Palma, De Niro, Schrader, etc. I knew them all and watched their careers skyrocket while I struggled along. Most of the time I didn't want to think about the possibility that being a woman was what was making it difficult to succeed. I had many male friends who were having a hard time too. Some of them never got anywhere, which is heartbreaking. I did start thinking about my gender once I got past about 45 because the industry does heavily discriminate when age and gender are combined. Also, that was about the time that the studio trend was to hire young, mostly inexperienced video and commercial directors so that they could control them. They didn't want older, experienced people like us who knew the rules and who had precedent-setting clauses in their contracts that gave agents the leverage to demand high salaries, final cut, and more creative control.

What are the most common pressures you've faced?

PS: Basically women have to work harder to be directors than men do. We cannot make mistakes. If we have a box-office flop, it's nearly impossible to get the next job. If we want our career to stay on track, we cannot get any bad publicity, or certainly cannot get arrested for drunk driving or drugs, etc., like male directors sometimes do. We cannot even be too outspoken. I always say that when a male director throws a tantrum, he is viewed as a genius. When a woman throws one, it must be that time of the month. For young women directors there's always that sexual pressure, unfortunately. Back when I had "Rock 'n Reel," my music video company, I worked for a lot of the big record companies. I was called to a hotel in Beverly Hills to meet with an executive one afternoon. When I got there he was totally drunk, made obnoxious advances, then he proceeded to tear off half my clothes. Although rather extreme and hopefully not that common, that was a pressure, let me tell you.

Film directors are notorious for being tough, demanding, and direct. From what I've heard from insider insight, a female film director, in order to make her presence and demands known, has to have an even stronger upper hand than a typical male film director. Is this true?

AA: Directing is not a matter of being tough and demanding, but knowing what you want and communicating. In fact, having directed many actors to award-nominated performances, I did very little. The real key to directing actors is creating safety for them to give you all they've got. It's hard to achieve that by being a dick. In terms of your crew, you will get their best by being respectful and communicating what you want. As far as being tough on getting final cut, I have tough people who negotiate that up front. For budget issues, I have producers who have my back. That's how everyone works. If you want to be a raving maniac on set, you can be, but most directors I know are not like that, male or female.

PS: Respect for a director on a set comes from different sources. Clearly one of the most important is her/his assertiveness and the ability to make a correct and quick decision. Over the years so many crew members have told me that they like to work with me because I know what I want. I answer their questions fast and efficiently because it helps them do their job better. If you say, "let me think about it" you are essentially just putting their work on hold. I don't think having a stronger upper hand than a male director is the way to get the work done. Charm, good intentions, and a positive approach go a long way. If a woman director gets too pushy or demanding, the point of diminishing returns kicks in a lot faster than when one of those male directors gets in a bad mood.

When making a movie, there are usually two visions involved — the director's and the producer's. Do you ever feel there is a tug-of-war involved with decision making and negotiating ideas, or do you feel there is usually a happy medium?

AA: Well, no. You need to work with a producer who protects your vision as director. And your producer should be the buffer between you and the studio or you and the financier. You will always have to listen to anyone who gives you even a dime to make your movie, but a good producer will filter those notes for you.

Any advice or last thoughts for future filmmakers and producers?

AA: Always be well into the next project before a film is released!

PS: Don't make violent, negative movies with themes about destruction and nihilism. There's enough of that in the real world already. Make films that are life-affirming and work toward making this world a better place.

Okay, back to talking about lady film directors and the final question we've been trying to get at.

Why are female film directors a rarity?

Plain and simple: I don't know. If I had talked to more people, I still don't think I would be anywhere near a conclusion. Everybody has a different story to tell, experiences learned, and a different way of doing things. Everybody has challenges. And down the road some may encounter discrimination, whether it's race, sexual orientation, age, or gender. I know I have to forever live with being a less-than-punk looking, skinny, white, hearing-impaired blonde chick . . . In the music industry, that's a challenge.

If you look at the Wikipedia site, there seems to be a very long list of female directors from all over the world. So is it really "lack of" or just plain ignorance? Maybe we're just not aware of who's doing what. It's all out there, so maybe we just need to look further. And more important — anything is possible. If you don't mind me getting a little new-agey on your asses, I wish all of you readers the best of luck. Replace the words "I can't" with "I can." And watch Troma's *LolliLove*. It's hilarious, it was directed by a woman, and there's a moral.[2]

Thank you Allison, Penelope, Lloyd and TROMA!
xoxo
Lindsey

---

[2]Dear Lindsey, there is a moral in *LolliLove* — director Jenna Fischer has said that after *LolliLove*, she never wants to direct another film. xoxo, LK*

*EDITOR'S NOTE: This has nothing to do with Fischer being female, and probably more to do with Lloyd's "acting" in *LolliLove* where he played a priest. Go figure . . .

Chapter five

Casting: Stick to Fish, Avoid the Toilet Seats

Once your production staff is assembled and your crew is in place, it's time to put together the motley crew of eager thespians that will bring your characters to life. Convincing people to audition for a film is pretty easy to do. After all, who didn't grow up fantasizing about being a movie star? Everyone wants to be in a movie, right? And that's exactly who will audition for your film — everyone. This is not as great as it may sound.

EENY, MEENY, MINY, MOE . . .

Casting your film is actually a lot like fishing. You throw out a line and hope that you don't reel in a bunch of mullets, sharks, or rusty toilet seats, instead of fish. Let me explain. Mullets are the folks who aren't really all that bad as far as people go, but their idea of "acting" seems to be just becoming a more exaggerated and pathetic version of themselves. You may end up using a few mullets to fill small roles, or as nonspeaking actor persons.[1] Just make sure they aren't actually sporting mullets, as this may date your film back to the 1920s, when

---

[1] We don't like the term "extra" because it indicates a class distinction on the set. To keep everyone equal, we refer to everyone (the stars, cameo roles, extras, etc.) as "actor persons."

mullets were cool. Sharks are far worse than mullets. Because they have fins and swim around, you may mistake them for fish. But they are, in fact, pure evil, and will destroy your movie with their sharp and slimy rows of teeth, also known as their egos and their negativity. Beware the shark diva. As for toilet seats, I think the name is self-explanatory. These people are, simply put, shit, and you don't want them in your film. Anytime you look at someone's resume or audition tape, ask yourself, "Is this person a fish?" Stick to casting fish,* and you're already on the road to making a better movie.

FIGURE 5.1 *Hundreds of Buffalo citizens showed up each day, for no money, to stand in the blistering sun on the set of* Poultrygeist: Night of the Chicken Dead. *Here, they pray for rain. But God hates Lloyd Kaufman.*

THE QUEST BEGINS

The first step in your casting quest will be to get your casting director[2] to make up some snazzy looking flyers with the words ACTORS WANTED splashed across the top. Include a brief description of what

---

*INDIGNANT FOOTNOTE GUY SAYS: For the record, I don't agree with catching fish for food or sport. Back when I was in school at the Modesto Technical College for Fine Print, I was secretary for an animal rights group called Writers Against the Nonessential Killing of Earth's Repressed Species (WANKERS).

[2]I use a smart** and organized PA, usually a movie set virgin, as my casting director.

**In Tromaville's casting department, "smart" means having an IQ above 85.

you are looking for; all of your contact information; whether any nudity will be required and whether the production is SAG or non-SAG (Screen Actors Guild). Then assign some skater kids to get these flyers plastered throughout your city. Try starting with your local college campus, video stores, theater groups, old age homes — anywhere where people are desperate . . . er . . . eager to break onto the big screen. You will also want to get this information posted on the World Wide Web. Ask any interested parties to please send in a resume and photo. Now you sit back and wait. Within days you will begin to receive a ton of submissions.

"Holy shit," you will think. "This is going to be a breeze. I'm going to have this movie cast[3] in no time!" This won't be the case. You see, every drama club reject from here to Timbuck-fucking-tu will consider themselves perfect for the job and will gladly send you their information. Go through their resumes with your casting director, look over their headshots and begin to organize them according to which parts you think they might be good for. If you need hot, young men for sex and nudity (in the film, that is[4]) you may want to set aside the most attractive looking hunks specifically for those roles.

LOVE IN THE TIME OF PHOTOSHOP

Exercise caution when going through the headshots, as most actors tend to lie. Sure, they might appear perfectly normal in their photo, but only after meeting them in person do you realize that the photo was taken around twenty years ago, before they started smoking crystal meth, bathing in pig grease, and eating Big Macs with cheese in their oatmeal. Luckily, with the advent of e-mail and the Internet, you can have the actors with the more promising headshots send you full-body shots and maybe even some videos. It's still no guarantee, but it's something. All I'm saying is, prepare to be disappointed in the selection. Once you have organized your submissions, it's time for phase two of the casting process: the almost-open call.

THE ALMOST-OPEN CALL

The almost-open call is the time when you will get almost every person in town with dreams of making it as an actor to come in and

---

[3]Or "casted."

[4]If it's not for the film, I recommend the Manhole Club on 9th Avenue.

  FOOTNOTE GUY'S RESPONSE: 9th Avenue and what? Do you know their hours?

strut his stuff for you. At Troma, we usually give auditioners around a minute to do whatever they want as we videotape them. This isn't as skeevy as it sounds. She can recite a poem, sing a song, deliver a monologue, or perform a magic trick — it's entirely up to her. Grab a smart[5] PA and be sure to film all auditions. This PA should get up and personal with your actor hopefuls, shooting them from various angles and distances. After all, you want to know how these folks look on screen. Also, use a boom mic[6] so you get decent sound.

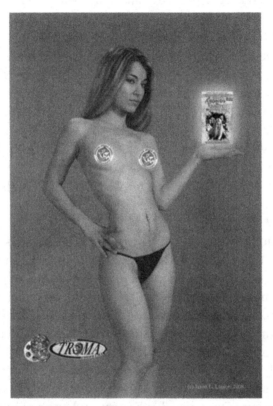

FIGURE 5.2A *Lloyd Kaufman is gratified when fans, such as Nicola Fiore, volunteer to dress (or undress) as Toxie or as Tromettes. This genuine loyalty gives him the strength to keep going.*

---

[5]In Tromaville's audio/visual department, "smart" means having an IQ higher than 60. "Smart" can also mean having his own video equipment.

[6]In Tromaville, a boom mic is a $19.99 plastic microphone attached with gaffer* tape to a boom stick held by a sweaty PA.

　*GAFFER — hey, that's another fishing term.

FIGURE 5.2B *Tromeo, Tromeo . . . Wherefore art thou Tromeo? Oh yeah, at DragonCon 2008!*

When your actors first arrive, have them all fill out a form for you that includes all the basic information you will need, such as name, age, height, contact information, etc. You should also ask them if nudity and sex scenes are a problem, thereby giving them another golden opportunity to lie to you. Allow them a space to list any special skills they may have, and if they have access to any out of the ordinary props or locations. All of this information will come in handy later on down the road.

Have them start off their audition by clearly stating their name and phone number into the camera. I know all of this is included in the form you just had them fill out, but when someone fucks up and loses all of the paperwork, you will still have a way to get in touch with this person. If your auditions are going to require any female nudity, I feel it wise to have a female staff person on hand to make them feel comfortable and reduce the risk of a frivolous sexual harassment claim later on. It's your word against hers when it all comes down to it, and the creepy geek sitting alone in a room with a video camera and a naked girl doesn't stand a chance in court. Mix and match your actors with other people to see how they work together as a team. Poke them with sticks. See if they flinch. (Just kidding on that last one).[7]

Obviously, it's pretty hard to tell whether someone is a good actor in only a minute's time. What you're looking for here is charisma, energy, and on-screen presence. Be mindful as to what characters you think will suit each actor. Somebody who makes you laugh your ass off in their audition might suck donkey balls when it comes time to deliver a dramatic performance. You will want to carefully go over all of these tapes with your casting director and primary crew. Take everyone's opinion into consideration, but remember — you have the final say when it comes down to which person will be portraying your characters.

JAMES GUNN KNOWS FUNNY

James Gunn is the writer/director of Slither *and writer of* Dawn of the Dead (2004). *He came to Tromaville to be Lloyd's personal assistant, but quickly realized that was a big mistake. After James masturbated on Lloyd's desk*, Lloyd immediately promoted him to writer of the Tro-masterpiece,* Tromeo & Juliet. *He now makes Lloyd call him Mr. Gunn.*

For me, one of the main things for directing comedies — or directing anything — is to be as overprepared as possible, and then go to set and be willing to let go of all of it. With comedy, it needs to feel fresh. Directing comedy is hard, and you don't always know what's funny on set. Sometimes things are getting big laughs from the crew and they aren't that funny. But I think being really prepared, but also willing to find those gems while you're shooting is really a big part.

When directing comedies, surround yourself with funny people. The actors in comedy are so important, more than anything else — more than in drama. In dramas, there are just so many dramatic things you can do with your camera to make people feel a certain way with the way something is cut, the way something is shot, etc. Editing can make a big difference with comedy, but it's hard to shoot something funny. It's a lot more important what the performances are like, and to be able to find those performances and keep them in the same place and make sure everybody's acting at the same level. Choosing the right people is huge. People really need to find what they're good at and do what they're good at. There are directors — people in general — who want to do comedy and

---

[7]I'm not entirely kidding.

*See *All I Need to Know About Filmmaking I Learned From The Toxic Avenger* for the whole sordid story.

they think they're funny and they're doing stand up comedy and they're out there and they're trying to be funny. They think they are the funniest person in the room. But their friends don't think they're the funniest person in the room and they've never been the funniest person in the room. I mean, if you're funny, you're funny. And certain people are.

I think you just have to listen to people laughing when you talk, and if they aren't laughing, then maybe another kind of film would be better suited to you.

FIGURE 5.3 James Gunn's hair, moments after an unfortunate contact with a live electrical wire.

FIGURE 5.4 James Gunn giggles at Lloyd Kaufman's unsuccessful attempt to throw himself under a bus.

MENTION JAMES GUNN A LITTLE MORE . . . PEOPLE LIKE THAT FUCKER

On *Tromeo & Juliet*, I stood my ground and fought for the lovely and talented Jane Jensen to play Juliet. This was much to the chagrin of James Gunn and Producer Andrew Weiner, who both felt that we needed someone with larger breasts to "fill" the role. Oddly enough, Jane was the first actress of hundreds to audition for Juliet; I knew immediately that she was the one.[8] I stuck to my guns and we wound up with a fabulous performance from an incredible actress.

The truth is, I am a giant pussy, and even though I wanted Jane, I eventually would have buckled under pressure from James and Andrew. Luckily, the gyno-actor person they favored proved to be a psycho bitch with an interfering creep of a manager, so James and

---

[8]I happen to prefer lithe, hard-bodied gynos with modest melons for my leading ladies. See *Terror Firmer* and *Poultrygeist* for more leading gynos with modest melons and hard, lithe, hard, hard bodies . . .*

*EDITOR'S NOTE: Lloyd and I were in the midst of discussing this footnote, but he seems to be taking an excessively long bathroom break here. I don't want to be crass, but come on, Kaufman.

Andrew, who now adore Jane too,[9] agreed to give her the part of Juliet. So I didn't really have to stick to my guns, but the lesson works much better that way.

THE TRUTH ABOUT ACTORS

Most of the people showing up for the open call won't be established or even professional actors. This is fine. In fact, I prefer working with first-time or non-actors in my films. Anyone who has been lucky enough to attend one of my "Make Your Own Damn Movie" Master Classes or be in line behind me at the deli has heard me say the following about a million times:

Most actors suck

The majority of people who consider themselves actors are talentless, pretentious fucks with overblown egos and some form of mild retardation.[10] That might sound a tad bit harsh, but it's the plain truth. Be prepared to sit through many painful auditions before you see anything even remotely resembling a decent performance. Of course, not all actors are this way — just most of them. From my 40 years personal experience I would venture to guess that approximately 1% of actors are genuinely talented, good people to work with and when you find them, this 1% will prove to be some of the greatest people in the world! Countless Troma stars including Sean Bowen of *Troma's War*, *Citizen Toxie's* Heidi Sjursen, Joe Fleishaker, who has appeared in tons[11] of Troma movies, Trey Parker and Matt Stone, and Oscar winner/non-Troma star Jon Voight (I could go on and on*) are

---

[9]Unfortunately, Jane may hate me. She refused to have anything to do with the 10th anniversary DVD of *Tromeo & Juliet*. She has also said that if Troma ever goes out of business or I croak, she would like to buy the negative of *Tromeo & Juliet* and make the whole thing go away. This, of course, fills me with pride as the film's director.

[10]And as you may have guessed by now, being considered mildly retarded in Tromaville is an accomplishment in itself.

[11]Joe also weighs close to a ton. Check out his many Troma credits on IMDB. Joe most recently exploded on screen in the now-acclaimed "explosive diarrhea scene" from *Poultrygeist*.

*EDITOR'S NOTE: Lloyd actually did go on and on here with a litany of actors' names, but I cut the list. This book needs to end up at 322 pages to fulfill the contract, but you're not going to fill it up that way Lloyd. Please don't resort to making lists. Also, I seriously doubt that you knew and were on friendly terms with Sarah Bernhardt.

100% decent, talented, and idealistic people who make life worth living. These are the people you want in your film. Having to sift through the other 99% to find them is the hard part. Have patience.

TRIMMING THE FAT (FIGURATIVELY, NOT NECESSARILY LITERALLY)

One of the main benefits of making a low-budget film is that I don't feel compelled to rush my movie out the door to meet some arbitrary release date. I can take as long as I want to make sure that things get done right. Believe me, when it comes to casting your film, you want to be able to take all of the time you need. If you have even the slightest reason to believe that someone is going to be a problem on the set — no matter how great an actor he may be — eliminate her now.

At Troma, we tend to make the audition process as difficult and grueling as humanly possible. We want our prospective actors to know right up front that filmmaking is an incredibly difficult process, especially on a low-budget film. The perks that actors tend to receive on a big studio film are nonexistent at Troma, and the hours are long. I figure that by making our auditions as hard as the shoot is going to be, we weed out those who can't cut it on the set. The only reason to want to be an actor in a Troma movie is to gain experience, perfect one's craft, and make some art. It sure ain't the money. I make sure of that. The self-absorbed have no place on the set of *un film de Lloyd Kaufman*.

BILL LUSTIG ON ACTING AND ACTORS

Take acting classes. I had an opportunity to go and it helped me to understand the process. Some of the best directors have some background in acting. Be honest with the actors. Don't try to sound super knowledgeable, and don't get into abstracts. You say "here's the scene, I want you to say the line and end up here by the windows." A good actor will take that and run with it. I've never had to fire an actor, but I left a film called *The Expert* because the star, Jeff Speakman, threatened to kill me. I had shot most of the film and he came to me during the violent climax and said he couldn't do it because he would be setting an example for the children of America. There was nothing I could do to persuade him. I wound up shooting the scene and manipulated it to look the way I wanted. Of course there is always a rat on the set and someone told him and a couple of days later he called me and the producers and wanted to see the footage. He came into the editing room and saw the change and he was a karate bullshit guy and he threatened to kill me, at which point I thought it was in my best interest to leave and head west. The final cut of the film has it the way I shot it. The funny part is he had a guy with him, a meek 130-lb, 5'4" guy, who showed up on set with a big bag of weapons. This was before 9/11 and the weapons were like *Soldier of Fortune* magazine. He showed me all the stuff and I was a little fascinated with this guy, who was clearly a little "off." One of the things he did was take out some knife and showed me how well-balanced it was and then he threw it into the couch sofa of my hotel room! I said to Jeff, "these are the type of people you're hanging out with?" Jeff had the IQ of a doorknob. I don't care if he finds me. What are you going to do, Lloyd, give him my address?

After you have gone through all of the taped auditions, make a pile of all the ones you found interesting but don't trash the rest. They may become valuable. If only we had saved the Super8 footage of Madonna, who auditioned for *The First Turn On!*, or Vincent D'Onofrio, who tried out for *The Toxic Avenger*, maybe I wouldn't have to be writing this damn book just to fund my next movie.[12]

THE HOLLERBACK ... ER ... THE CALLBACK

It's now time for the callback. This is when you "call back" all of the actors you feel might work out in your film. From this point on, the audition will take on a more structured approach. When you have your actors come in for the callbacks, have them read pages from your script. If you're lucky, they will be interested enough to want the pages in advance. Have extra copies made for this purpose and encourage them to get "off book"[13] for the callback.

During your callbacks, play mix-and-match with your actors, placing them in different groups so you can see how well they play

---

[12]EDITOR'S NOTE: Hey, Lloyd, you're the one who asked me for the book deal. If you want out, I would be happy to consider it.

LLOYD'S RESPONSE: Did I say "damn book?" I meant damn fine, Ma'am. And finely edited at that.

[13]"Off book" refers to knowing one's lines without needing the script. If you find an actor who can be off book by the second audition, don't let him in the building. He's obviously a pretentious asshole. In fact, just send him over to Troma.

with others. You want to find that perfect combination that results in on-screen chemistry. Be sure to observe how well they get along outside of the audition too. Remember to keep videotaping all of your auditions, and get all the auditioners to sign actor releases. These tapes can serve as great bonus material on the DVD of your film, and you haven't even paid anyone yet!

Make sure that your actors know what time they need to arrive at the callback and you can probably eliminate from consideration anyone who is tardy. People who can't keep appointments are not to be trusted! If they can't make a simple audition on time, there is no way in hell they can be relied upon to show up on time every day to the set. Yeah, I know that life can get in the way of things from time to time. But unless they show up to your audition caked in blood after delivering a baby in an elevator, they have no excuse for being late.[14]

You may think this is a little extreme, but I find it perfectly reasonable. In fact, I will always choose the more reliable, dedicated individual over someone who may be a slightly better actor but who has less loyalty and work ethic. Considering the amount of time you'll be spending with the actors on your set, I think you will agree that the ability to act well isn't as important as the willingness to get shit done and not be a pain in your ass. Someday, when you're a big shot, you'll be able to afford people who can act AND not be a pain in your ass, but until that day, prioritize. While shooting *Citizen Toxie*, my actors took to late night partying, which resulted in lots of time lost the next day. Rather than chastise or fire the culprits, I lost my nerve, and wound up with some serious problems later on.[15] See, I told you I was a giant pussy. It would serve you well to learn from my mistakes. During *Poultrygeist*, however, Gabe Friedman, Kiel Walker, and Andy Deemer courageously fired and drove away the boozers and the druggies. By the time we started rehearsals, nobody stayed out late doing anything, much less drinking.[16]

---

[14]Actually, if they do arrive caked in blood, start filming! I'm sure you'll be able to fit it in the movie somewhere, and it's free!

[15]You can observe these hung over jerks, as well as several of my character flaws, up close and personal in *Apocalypse Soon: The Making of Citizen Toxie*, available now from www.troma.com. BUY TROMA!!

[16]In part because we had 20-hour shooting days and our location was in the middle of the Buffalo, New York, ghetto.

LET'S TALK SOME MORE ABOUT NUDITY...

If any roles require nudity, you need to have your actresses (and actors) disrobe on camera at some point. Your auditioners may sound all gung-ho about being naked on film at first, but many will chicken out when it comes time to actually do it. Better they do it now rather than on the day of the actual shoot. Some will try to convince you that they are uncomfortable doing it now during the rehearsal, but they will have no problem getting naked later on. These people are full of shit. You need to know up front who is willing to take off his clothes. If someone really has a problem with it, either get rid of her or find a different role for her to play. When we move on to set management, we'll discuss a little bit more about how nudity issues can fuck you over, but for now, let's just say that, if nudity is a part of your movie, be sure that everyone knows that. Enough said?*

JAMES GUNN KNOWS LLOYD KAUFMAN

It's really simple why Troma doesn't get any respect. Troma is completely vulgar. It's completely lowbrow. There's no doubt that Troma revels in being lowbrow and in being vulgar, and, that, throughout history, has never been the thing that is going to get any respect. It's really that simple, I mean, when you have farting and a shitload of gore and naked women, it's not always going to get the greatest attention from the masses or from the critics.

I think the Troma style of directing, and by "Troma style of directing" I mean the Lloyd Kaufman style of directing, works for Troma, and it would probably work almost nowhere else. For one, Lloyd is TRULY a director/producer. I mean, when he is directing, the production is on his mind, just as much as directing, if not more. Because Lloyd was the first director I really had intimate contact with and was around all the time — on *Tromeo & Juliet* we were next to each other twenty-four hours a day — I imprinted on him a lot and took on a lot of those traits. Producers love me for it, and studios like me because I'm always thinking about going over budget, I'm always thinking about the day going over and going into overtime, I'm always thinking about all these production things. People never talk about that part of it when they talk about the Troma style of directing. They never concentrate on how much of a producer Lloyd is when he's directing. And that's the reason why he's crazy. He doesn't get crazy because of

*A NOTE FROM YOUR LONELY FOOTNOTE GUY: Actually, Lloyd, could you talk a little more about the nudity. I kind of enjoyed that.

the directing; he gets crazy because of the producing. He's usually not getting upset because somebody's performance isn't good enough, for example. In fact, on a Troma movie, you'll see that the good actors are few and far between, in terms of a good performance, but you'll notice that everyone else acts like Lloyd. That's because Lloyd doesn't really know how to talk to actors how a director does. He "shows" actors how to act, so everybody on a Troma movie is usually doing a bad imitation of Lloyd, which ends up in this very, very strange aesthetic of a Troma movie that focuses on a lot of people making Lloyd faces all the time.

FIGURE 5.5 James Gunn and Elizabeth Banks on the set of *Slither*, just moments after walking in on Lloyd Kaufman in a compromising position with a prop reindeer.

BRINGING IT ALL TO A RAPID BOIL

You've got your production team. You've got your film crew. You even have a group of actors willing to tackle your movie with all their heart and soul. You might start to feel pretty good about yourself. After all, look at what you've accomplished thus far! But hey buddy, the preproduction ride isn't over yet. Now that you've got all these people hanging on your every word, you need to have something to say. As in, a plan.

Do you have a plan yet?

I didn't think so.

Turn the fucking page and we'll figure that out next. Let's go!

Chapter six

Preparation and Scheduling: Who Knew There Was So Much Paper Involved in the Art of Directing?

Okay. At this point, let's take a deep breath and evaluate our position. You're on the couch, I'm on top of you. . . . We're good. But what about your movie? Have you forgotten about that? Lucky for you, Uncle Lloydie is here to guide you through the most tedious of all the chapters — THIS ONE!

HOW TO KEEP HANDS BUSY (AND AWAY FROM YOUR CROTCH)

As the director of a film, your crew expects you to have somewhat of a clue. When there is a problem, yo, you need to solve it. If there is a question, you need to have the answer. One of the great things about being a director is that, while you can surround yourself with intelligent and qualified workers, you are the final authority on

103

everything. Everything! The downside to being a director, however, is often that you're the final authority on everything. Everything! So your most important task, aside from pointing the camera and yelling "action," is to be prepared. As prepared as fucking Girl Scouts.[1]

BREAKDOWNS (AS IN SCRIPT, NOT MENTAL . . . HOPEFULLY)

Now that you have a completed script, you need to go through it page by page and break it all down so that you can begin to work out your shooting schedule. Keep in mind that the method of breaking down a script detailed in this book is the way that I choose to do it, not necessarily the way other directors do it. (I would imagine that the way other directors do it is considered the right way.) I believe that my particular method happens to work best on a low-budget, independent film.

To break down the script properly, it helps if you have intimate knowledge of the story. Since you just so happen to be the individual who wrote the story,[2] nobody is better suited to break it down than you. In fact, I think the director should always be one of those who do the script breakdown.[3] This ensures that you will always know what the hell is supposed to be going on. Your production manager should also go through the process, as should the assistant director, but you can't rely on someone else to take this as seriously as you do. Often, production managers just hand the assignment off to an assistant, ensuring that nobody really has any idea what the hell is going on. In my opinion, neither the production manager nor the assistant directors[4] on *Terror Firmer* were familiar with the script breakdown. This proved to be a major problem. However, the situation did provide opportunity for some vintage Kaufman freakouts, which you can see and laugh at in *Farts of Darkness: The Making of Terror Firmer.*

---

[1] I don't endorse fucking Girl Scouts. Unless it is in exchange for Thin Mints.

[2] What follows is even more important if you, the director, did NOT write the script.

[3] If you're having trouble "doing" the script breakdown, don't worry . . . it happens to every guy sometimes. If you're a gyno and reading this book, and you're having trouble "doing" the script breakdown, maybe you should try growing a penis. It will instantly make you a much more successful director!

[4] If you watch *Fart of Darkness: The Making of Terror Firmer* you begin to wonder if the Assistant Director even read the script before filming began. Check it out on the 2-disc *Terror Firmer* DVD, available now from http://www.troma.com. BUY TROMA!

I like to break down my scripts three times: according to scenes, locations, and characters.[5] With scripts, the first breakdown is by scene. You write the scene number and then have columns for characters, location, costumes, props, miscellaneous, and special effects.

Scene 1	Location	Character	Costumes	Props	Misc. & Sp. FX
	Toxie's dump	Toxie	Tu-Tu	Mop	3-ft. penis monster
		Sarah	Naked	Blind cane	Smoke from nether regions
		Bill Clinton	Pants with zipper	Blue dress	Stain remover

Next, take a sheet of paper and write "locations" across the top. Then draw six columns down the sheet, each with labels of their own: location, scene numbers, characters, props, costumes, and miscellaneous. Once you have your sheet ready (this is going to take a whole lot of paper, so you may want to pilfer* a few stacks from the bottom of a copy machine at Kinko's) you can set about going through your script page by page and breaking down each location.

When you're done, you'll have a complete chart with each and every location listed, showing you what characters are needed for that location, what props you will need for that location, the costumes your characters are going to be wearing at that location, and any miscellaneous information regarding that particular location. The miscellaneous column is where I list any special effects, stunts, or actor persons we will be using at that particular time and useful reminders to myself to pick up cheese and fat-free milk on the way home. Following this same basic method, I then create a similar chart for all of the characters in the movie. I like to break the characters down as follows: character name, scene number, locations, costumes, props, and miscellaneous. This is going to result in a lot of unused paper,[6] as not every character is going to be appearing in every scene.

---

[5]I also like to break my actors down emotionally at least three times. It makes them more receptive to the guilt trips and histrionics I'll need to pull later on.

*EDITOR'S NOTE: Focal Press and its parent company, Reed Elsevier, in no way endorse the theft of copy paper from Kinko's, or any other copy service. Please don't sue us.

[6]Al Gore may brand you public enemy number one, but Al Gore's never made a movie... Well, he has never made a good movie!

This is tedious, but it's not fucking rocket science. And trust me, it's worth it. By breaking down the script in this fashion, I can pretty much commit the entire breakdown to memory, and I have a quick reference to exactly what I need at my fingertips. It was while working on *Joe*[7] that I learned from Production Manager George Manasse that whoever broke down the script held the most vital knowledge[8] on the set. It might as well be you. You can then have your production manager create a snazzier looking version based on yours. There are computer programs that will do this for you, but I would warn against using them. The program might be able to tell you what you need on any certain day, but it can't account for how much time you need to allocate to each particular scene. This is something you can only plan out by doing the breakdown by hand. In an age of computers and programs, this may seem stupid but I find that by doing this exercise by hand, all the details in the script get indelibly printed on my brain; later this nuts and bolts knowledge gives me the confidence and wherewithal to improvise wildly when we are actually on set filming.

By having a well-prepared script breakdown, you'll be able to work out a realistic shooting schedule. Remember that everything will take a hell of a lot longer to shoot than you might think. Special effects shots and stunts can each eat up several days, so don't schedule other scenes to be shot along with them unless you're absolutely confident that the pyrotechnics for your exploding prostate shot are going to work the first time out. (Hint: they won't.) Also keep in mind the amount of time that it will take to apply any complicated makeup before the cameras can even get rolling. It took an average of three or four hours every day to get Dave Mattey into his Toxie makeup on *Citizen Toxie*. This all has to be taken into consideration when hashing* out your shooting schedule.[9]

---

[7] *Joe* (1970) was an independent NYC movie directed by John G. Avildsen and introduced Peter Boyle, Susan Sarandon, and moi to 35 mm films. It cost $150,000 and Norman Wexler's script got an Oscar nomination. This could never happen today.

[8] If you ever get the opportunity to intern or PA on a movie, even a shitty kabillion dollar movie starring the Jonas Brothers, break the script down. No one will ask you to do this, but it's a great exercise and learning experience. The intimate knowledge you gain will translate into power at some point when director Brett Ratner sees that you know more about the script than his production manager.

*FRIENDLY FOOTNOTE GUY SAYS: I haven't seen the word "hash" used since I footnoted Timothy Leary's memoirs. There was a lot of talk about hash there.

[9] Your makeup people will eventually get the process down to a science, and not so much time will be required as principal photography progresses.

FIGURE 6.1 *George Romero doesn't appreciate where Lloyd Kaufman's right hand is headed.*

A NOTE FROM MY EDITRIX

---------------------------Original Message---------------------------

From: elinor@repress.com
Sent: July 11, 2008 4:26 PM
To: Lloyd Kaufman <lloyd@troma.com>
Subject: a few ideas

Lloyd,

Coming along quite well. Still waiting to see some of that Lloyd Kaufman directing magic!

P.S. Love the chart in Chapter 4. Let's try some more practical things like that? I'm really just not seeing a lot of focus here. . .

Best,
Elinor

Sent via BlackBerry by AT&T

---------------------------End Message---------------------------

MENTION YALE A FEW TIMES — PEOPLE RESPECT THAT

My editor feels that, at this point, the book is becoming a bit dry and suggests that I put a few personal details in. I thought talking about my scabies would be considered personal, but what do I know? Let's try something different.

While at Yale, I majored in Chinese Studies and fell under the influence of Taoism — you know, yin and yang.

Having a very low budget sucks (yang) because you have to sleep on the floor, eat cheese sandwiches three times a day and learn how to defecate in a paper bag. But, and it's a big but, there is a *yin*! (See? That Yale degree really IS of some use!)

SCREW YOU, MR. MARX

Screen Actors Guild rules make it almost impossible to film in sequence. On a union shoot, if you use an actor on Monday and then don't film her again until Thursday, you still must pay her the union rate for Tuesday and Wednesday, even though she was just sitting around cleaning her ears.[10]

However, since there are no union rules to screw up *your* schedule, you CAN film in sequence. With *Poultrygeist*, the entire cast was asked to live on location for almost 10 weeks. That way, we could use them whenever we needed them. They were paid small lump sums for the entire shoot. We didn't have to pay them while they hung around, no matter how well hung they were . . . or how clean their ears became.

FILMING IN SEQUENCE — JOYCEAN EPIPHANY

As a director, being able to film in sequence is a miraculous advantage. By filming the script in its order, you can re-write, expand the parts of actors who excel, kill off a character if the actor is uncooperative or in any way resembles a shithead; you can even re-write the ending if you shoot it later in the schedule or at the end. Also, for young inexperienced actors, shooting the beginning and the middle before the ending of your script makes life a lot less confusing and will help them to give much better performances.[11]

---

[10]Or complaining about having to sit around. Get the irony?

[11]Shooting in sequence may not work for dyslexic actors, however.

Obviously if you have lots of locations, you can't keep moving back and forth between the same locations as "company moves" are very time-consuming. *Poultrygeist* pretty much took place in and around the American Chicken Bunker restaurant set, so we did film in sequence. This still meant that we had to light the kitchen, film there, then light the dining room and film there, then hump the equipment back to the kitchen[12] and re-light, etc. This is a real pain for the crew, but it sure was clucking cool to be able to film the end of the film on the last day of principal photography!

Be as flexible as possible regarding your shooting schedule. If your production is anything like a Troma production, you'll be constantly changing and re-writing your script on the fly. You need to give yourself enough breathing room to account for all of the changes to come, as inspiration for new scenes and characters can strike at any moment. This makes it more important than ever that you, your production manager, and your assistant directors are all on the same page regarding scheduling and re-writes.

CAN I TALK ABOUT NUDITY YET?

Remember how I said that people will flake out when it comes to nudity, no matter how hard you grill them during the audition process? Well, my single major piece of advice regarding your shooting schedule, aside from shooting your scenes in order, is to not shoot your scenes entirely in order. SHOOT ALL OF YOUR SEX SCENES AND NUDITY AT THE BEGINNING OF PRODUCTION. This will guarantee that the groups of hard-bodied young actors you have assembled don't decide to flake out on you later when it comes time to expose their naughty bits for the entire world to gawk at. In other words, you can avoid situations like this:

> "I've decided that I don't want to do any nudity," declares the young actress.
>
> "But this is a sex scene. Nudity is a large part of that," responds the kindly director.

---

[12]Why didn't we keep the kitchen lit? Why did we re-light every time we moved back in? That is because I'm an idiot.*

*FOOTNOTE GUY SAYS: Lloyd, you really need to stop making so many self-deprecating jokes. You are one of my favorite film directors, whose influence pervades the work of so many of today's mainstream directors — Quentin Tarantino, Takashi Miike, Ben Stiller . . . You had to keep re-lighting because you couldn't afford more than three lights. There is no shame in that!

"I know, but I have a boyfriend now and he doesn't want me to do it."

"I can appreciate your situation, but you've already committed to doing this. Remember when you auditioned and I asked you if you minded nudity? Remember when you said you would do it? Remember when you auditioned naked . . . and rehearsed naked? Remember how we're shooting this scene today?" asks the slightly worried director.

"I remember. But I'm not doing it. Besides, you've been filming me for the past month. What are you going to do if I quit . . . start over?

The excessively worried director chews on his lip.

"Your boyfriend knows it's just a movie, right? I mean, he knows you're not actually going to be having sex with this guy."

"Fuck you, Kaufman. I'm not doing it."

At this point, the man, previously known as the director, realizes that he is fucked and proceeds to blow his brains out.

Even if your actors have promised you that they will have no problem at all going buff in your film, something is bound to happen to fuck it all up. I've had actresses go nude during taped rehearsals, and then turn around and refuse to do the exact same thing when it came time to shoot the actual scene. If you shoot these scenes first,[13] you can easily replace any of the actors who chicken* out immediately. It's not so easy to replace them if half the film is in the can.

SHOOTING UP: SOME HELPFUL TERMS TO GET YOU STARTED

If you're anything like me, you probably never stepped foot in a film school.[14] Therefore, I have decided to devote a portion of this insightful chapter on *preparation* to a few filmmaking terms that may prove useful to you. I'm not going to go through every single directorial option and piece of movie-making nomenclature here,

---

[13] With *Poultrygeist*, Gabe Friedman and I decided to take this one step further and not only shoot the nude scenes first, but also put the nude scenes first in the movie. That way we could also shoot in sequence! However, putting nudity, butt plugs, and fisting into the first scene of a film often causes critics and audiences to walk out in the first five minutes . . . Lesson learned!

*FOOTNOTE GUY SAYS: *Poultrygeist* sure did stay in Lloyd's brain — all those chicken references! Omeletting you know! Ha ha, footnote chicks love my clucked up sense of humor. Are there any women out there who want to meet me on the 5th bench in Central Park at the 65th St. entrance?

[14] You probably also have an addiction to Alsup's chimichangas and midget porn as well.

because frankly, I usually end up calling everything, "you know, that thing . . . you piece of shit . . . you know what I mean!"

- **The Shot**: Not to be confused with the trip to the free clinic after a late night of boozing that makes it burn when you pee, the shot is the fundamental fixture of making a film.

- **Storyboards**: If you or someone you know has a knack for drawing, you may want to take the time to storyboard your scenes before filming them. Storyboarding is basically pre-planning your shots by creating a sort of comic book to serve as a visual blueprint for your movies. If done well enough, you can pull off your shots in a fraction of the time, since you already know exactly what you need for that particular scene, reducing the need for too much coverage. Storyboards are great, but I don't usually use them. That well thought out and storyboarded shot might not work out exactly as you had hoped and production can't come to a screeching halt while you figure something else out. I generally only use them for stunts and complicated special effects, especially if multiple cameras are used. If you lack any artistic ability whatsoever, there are computer programs available that provide a cut-and-paste method of putting together your storyboards. Of course, these cost money. If you can have someone draw them for you for free, I say let them.

STUART GORDON ON STORYBOARDING

I tend to do storyboards for special effects sequences. I know some directors storyboard everything, like the Coen brothers supposedly storyboard every single shot in their movies. But I just storyboard the ones that involve special effects or stunts. Even if you're not a terrific artist, storyboards are helpful — even if you just draw stick figures. Hitchcock was one of the first directors to really use storyboards and he storyboarded his entire films. Hitchcock used to say that when he finished storyboarding the movie, the movie was done in his mind, and that shooting it was just a technicality.

On movies where there is a bigger budget, sometimes I'll bring in an artist to help me. I work very closely with those artists. I don't just turn them loose and let them come back with how they would shoot the scene. I want them to draw me the shots I am planning to use.

FIGURE 6.2 Stuart Gordon doing his famous Mr. T impersonation.

One of the things I've learned is that in moviemaking, no matter if the budget is enormous or small, you still have the same problems and it's the same process. There really is no difference between working on a tiny, little independent movie, or on a Troma film, and working on some huge, gigantic, blockbuster, $100 million movie. You're always dealing with the same issues — time and money. I was working on a film and I had a storyboard artist who had worked with Spielberg on *Raiders of the Lost Ark*. We had been storyboarding for a while and one day he called and said "I can't come in today." I asked why and he said "Spielberg needs me to come back and do some storyboarding for this *Raiders of the Lost Ark* thing." He told me there was a sequence it turned out they couldn't afford. That made me feel really good. Even Steven Spielberg can't afford to do everything that he wants to do.

ELI ROTH SAYS . . . (TO STORYBOARD OR NOT TO STORYBOARD. . .)

I don't storyboard because I find that once you get to your location, your shots change. Starting out, I obsessively tried to line up my storyboards and my shots to look the same. When I worked with David Lynch, one of the things he really, really taught me was to shoot what is in front of the frame. Look at the frame and what's in front of it. Don't just look at what is in your head and try to force it into that. Say "okay, this is what is in my head, but this is what I actually have to work with. What's there? Is there something better? Is there something different? Does something really need to be changed? Does it not?"

- **Framing a Shot**: This basically involves pointing the camera at your actors and positioning everything so that they look good on the screen. When filming dialogue, it's important to block your actors so that you can actually tell your characters apart and distinguish who is actually doing the talking. Believe me, I have seen more than my fair share of films where the director must have thought "blocking" meant physically blocking the view of the audience. Having your actor's back to the camera while she is talking is generally not a good idea. And you can bet your ass that blocking the view of any onscreen female nudity is a cinematic death wish. Take a look at *The Good, The Bad and the Ugly* (or any film by Sergio Leone for that matter) to see some of the most beautifully framed shots put to film. Also, *Danger! Diabolik* by Mario Bava has some very interesting shots and framing that serve as inspiration.[15]

- **Master**: Your master shot is the shot that establishes the location and position of the characters in the scene. It used to be that the master shot was the most important shot of the scene, with all of the other shots directly relating back to the master. However, some members of the new generation of directors are so hopped up on cocaine, and their brains have been so fried by MTV-style editing, that the traditional use of

---

[15]The Coen brothers' comic masterpiece *Burn After Reading* introduces Frances McDormand's character by showing her stomach blubber first. You don't see her face for at least six lines of dialogue — sheer genius!

the master has gone the way of the dodo on most films. This can be a problem if you don't know what you're doing, as it creates a mass of confusion on the screen. But as I've said, there are no rules to this game. With action sequences, a good technique is to play the entire scene out in the master a few times, and then intercut the master with all of your coverage. This provides the audience with a good sense of where all of the characters are, and the action will unfold in a logical manner. Your spectacularly staged fight sequence[16] won't mean a hill of rat shit if nobody can tell what is going on. I suggest you take the time to watch *The Seven Samurai* by the legendary Akira Kurosawa in order to get an idea of well-used master shots. The Toxie/Evil Kabukiman fight scene in *Citizen Toxie* is a good one to deconstruct regarding master shot, coverage and handheld coverage.[17]

- **Two Shot**: You know those shots in a movie where two characters are talking to each other and we see them side by side from the waist up? That's a two shot. I would suggest not using too many of these in your film. Especially if you are shooting on digital video, as this will tend to make your shots look like home movies. If you decide to ignore this advice and use a lot of two shots anyway, you better make sure your dialogue is top notch. Take a look at some Kevin Smith films to see some well-used two shots. Otto Preminger's *Bonjour Tristesse* also has some awesome long cinemascope dialogue two shots where the actors[18] are absolutely brilliant.

- **Reverse Shot**: Let's say you are shooting a basic shot of two people having a conversation with each other. When you switch angles to look at whoever is doing the talking, but from the listener's point of view, this is called a reverse shot.[19]

---

[16] I use two cameras for fight master shots and then use handheld cameras to cover each punch, kick, etc.

[17] *Direct Your Own Damn Movie* Tip #282.5: Most stunt masters will suggest filming punches to the face with the back of the victim's head in frame and the fist coming toward the camera. This is what I usually do. However, in *Burn After Reading*, when John Malkovich socks Brad Pitt, his fist goes away from the camera. The effect is terrific and hilarious because you get to see Brad Pitt's goofy facial expressions!

[18] Jean Seberg, one of the stars of *Bonjour Tristesse*, subsequently offed herself. Some people blame the two shot, but personally, I blame the pills and the twenty-two shots of whiskey.

[19] This can also refer to the vomit produced after a night of heavy boozing.

By intercutting your two shot with plenty of reverse shots, you help keep the scene interesting. Usually these shots should match.

- **Crossing the Line**: When you shoot two people having a conversation, imagine an invisible line connecting them to each other, and then keep your camera on one side of this line when shooting your reverse shots. If you cross the line and shoot your characters from different sides, it will appear as if they are facing the exact same direction. It gets even worse if they are walking while talking. Crossing the line makes it look as though they are walking away from each other. This will confuse the audience and make you look like a rank amateur. And believe me, I know what rank amateur films look like. I make them for a living. Coincidentally, I have been accused of crossing the line many, many times.

- **Angles**: Just shooting someone straight on can get pretty boring. Kind of like this section of the book. . . .* You will want to mix up the look of your film by employing some interesting looking angles. A small ladder can be used to get different perspectives on each scene. You are limited only by your imagination! Check out any Alfred Hitchcock film for brilliant high angle shots.

- **Coverage**: Coverage is what you call everything you need to shoot for any given scene. This includes close-ups, the master, the reversals, cutaway shots, everything. Not getting enough coverage can come back to gnaw on your scrotum like an angry gerbil, so I recommend going over each and every shot far enough in advance so that you can have a pretty good idea as to exactly how much coverage you're going to need. If you fail to get enough coverage during your shoot, you will have a hard time telling your story in a visually stimulating fashion. If you do fuck up, you can always "create" extra coverage by carefully utilizing footage from unused takes. Also, to be safe, "cutaway" shots like close-ups of hands, feet, or some other meaningful prop can save you in editing if coverage is lacking. You should also budget

---

* EDITOR'S NOTE: Actually, Lloyd, I am enjoying this part quite a bit. There is actually a small amount of useful information buried here.

and schedule a few "pick-up" days at the end of your shoot, so that you can go back and pick-up any shots you needed that you failed to get during the original schedule.[20] I leave some money in the budget so I can film a day or two during post production, after we have a rough cut. For *Terror Firmer*, when I saw the rough cut, I felt the chaos scene on Larry Benjamin's movie set was unclear, so we filmed more connecting shots and details. When we looked at the rough cut of *Citizen Toxie*, it became clear that all the scenes with television reporters sucked (my fault, not the actors). One evening in Minnesota, I happened to meet television twins, The Sklar Brothers, and we reshot all the reporter scenes with them about six months after principal photography. These scenes are some of the funniest[21] in *Citizen Toxie*.

- **Dolly**: A dolly is a wheeled device that you can mount your camera on and get nice, smooth flowing shots. Be prepared to shell out a ton of cash if you are hell-bent on getting a professional grade dolly. Fortunately, anything with a set of wheels that you can strap a camera onto is a perfectly usable dolly: a baby stroller, a skateboard, a wheelchair, you name it. A quick Internet search for "DIY camera dolly" will bring up a ton of online instructions that will walk you through the process of building your own dolly for around $50 in materials.

- **Tracking Shot**: The tracking shot is also known as a dolly shot or trucking shot. This shot gets its name from the fact that the camera is mounted on a dolly and then placed on a set of tracks so that it can smoothly follow the action. Some of the longest tracking shots on film can be seen in Wes Anderson's *The Darjeeling Limited*.[22] The first widely

---

[20] Budgeting for these "pick-up" days doesn't refer to the budget you need to set aside to pick-up hookers for the wrap party.

[21] Probably because I didn't direct these scenes. Gabe Friedman, our supervising editor, directed!*

  *FRIENDLY FOOTNOTE GUY SAYS: There you go, putting yourself down again Lloyd. Do you need a back rub?

[22] With Steadicam equipment, one can now "track" without using tracks. In 1976 I was on the set of *Rocky* when Garret Brown, the inventor of the Steadicam, filmed Stallone running up the museum stairs. This first use of Steadicam was almost as exciting as Thomas Edison's discovery of the iPod back in 1998!

released film to utilize this shot may have been the classic silent movie *Cabiria*, directed by Giovanni Pastrone.[23] Because of this, tracking shots were originally referred to as "Cabiria movements." Even though many smaller films prior to *Cabiria* used tracking shots, the technique was employed so well by Pastrone that the name stuck. This is a common occurrence in the filmmaking world. For example, the greatly underutilized cinematic technique of leaving the lens cap on while shooting a scene is known as the "Kaufman shot" in many filmmaking circles.

FIGURE 6.3 *In a shocking and unprecedented reversal, the chicken chokes Lloyd Kaufman.*

A clever way to pull off the tracking shot was shown to me by Mark Neveldine, director of *Crank* and the big-budget action flick *Game*. Mark likes to strap on a set of rollerblades and glide in and out of the action as it unfolds, getting very up close and personal while creating the illusion of an expensive tracking shot. I only recommend that you do this if you can actually operate a camera on a set of rollerblades without breaking your neck. Remember you are risking your physical well-being, and more importantly, you might shatter your camera or one of those kabillion dollar Cooke lenses

---

[23]Not to be confused with Moishe Pastrami, who invented the pastrami on rye sandwich and the atom bomb.

on the pavement when you fall on your ass. If all else fails, grab Grandma's wheelchair, throw your DP in the seat, and roll it along on a few pieces of plywood for a smooth shot.

Using these professional terms helps your crew to see you as the professional that you are. Or at least the professional that you may one day become. Using these terms may also help your crew to see you as a pretentious asshole, so use them wisely. As far as looking professional, you may also want to hold up your thumb and forefinger up in front of your face and squint through them as though you were envisioning a shot. This can also help you intimidate unruly crew members, as they may start to believe that you can crush their head from afar with just your fingers and your giant pretentious asshole mind.

JACK BERANEK

Jack Beranek is a beautiful young boy who took Lloyd's advice and made his own damn movie. Lloyd felt bad about that and offered Jack the opportunity to write this sidebar.

If anything, I am an example that *anyone* can get out there and make his or her own damn movie. I was a 16-year-old junior in high school living in a small town in southern Minnesota when I began working on my first full length feature film, and a few days past 17 when we actually began filming. If I can make a movie, so can you. You just have to be willing to actually start.

If you live in a small town about as far away from the film world as you can get, like I did, you might be wondering how the hell you do exactly start.

First of all, you might have to be willing to do the actual filming in another city where there are more people and options. One of the main reasons for this is that if there are a good amount of actors, crew members, etc., from another area, they will probably be much more willing to participate in your project if you travel to them, instead of vice versa. This was definitely the case for me.

Every state has a film commission, and every film commission has a website. If you don't already know of or have actors to be in your film, check out your state's film commission website for casting information. Better yet, see if your state has any websites or message boards that allow you to post ads for movie projects and casting calls. Even if you don't get a lot of responses, you might meet someone who will be the key to the rest of the movie. For my film *Health Freaks*, I went to MNTalent.com, a Minnesota-based website for film and television talent, and posted a casting call. Through this

FIGURE 6.4 Lloyd Kaufman, dressed as a waiter, mentors young man–boy director Jack Beranek on how to toss salad.

call I met Matthew Feeney who, as well as being a perfect choice for one of our lead roles, had countless connections in the Twin Cities film community, and he helped us cast the remaining roles as well as find the 75 extras and crew members needed for the movie.

When it comes to crew members, friends are always a good place to look. However, I would only recommend this if you have friends who are just as passionate about filmmaking as you are. Your friends might be helpful in drawing penises and other genitalia on you when you're passed out, but unless they dig movies as much as you do, you run the risk of them treating your project as a fuck around session instead of a real-life film set.

If you have trouble finding a crew, get creative and head to local camera stores, tech stores, etc., to find people who may have experience in the field. You'd be surprised at the amount of people who have experience behind cameras or working with lights and who are now working in stores to support themselves.

If your film calls for lots of blood and gore you'll probably want to find some help with bringing this stuff to life. Yes, there's tons of gory recipes you can make from scratch around your kitchen (which I'd recommend doing for as many of the effects as you can to save on the budget), but if your masterpiece calls for effects beyond your ability to create, you'll probably want to find someone with a little more experience. Also, check out websites for help and ideas on how to pull off some of the effects. There are tons of message boards (The Effects Lab is a good one) where people come together and discuss different ways to pull off effects, and it was a big help for some of the stuff in *Health Freaks*.

Locations can be another challenge. When looking for your location, try to avoid places owned by major retailers and conglomerates, and aim more for smaller, locally owned places. The big boys will take you through a lot more trouble like insurance, higher costs, or might just shut the door in your face. With mom and pop places, you're dealing with people who will hopefully be excited at the thought of a film being shot at their location. Throw out the possibilities of putting their names in the opening credits or on the film's website.

Lloyd might disagree here, but when you're not paying your cast or crew, one of the most important things to put effort into is making sure you have good food on set. And yes, Lloyd, the *good* part is essential. On the *Health Freaks* set, my mom actually prepared the food (things might have been different if she knew the movie had heads being impaled with mutated penises), and she always had a few card tables set up in a back room where the cast who were not currently working could eat and take a break. At 2:30 a.m., nothing can keep actors and crew members happier than some good food to munch on. It'll keep all the stoned extras quiet and satisfied. I cannot stress enough how important quality food is on a movie set, and I GUARANTEE that your cast and crew will be much happier and much more willing to work long and stressful hours for you if, at the very least, you provide them with good munchies.

As far as actually directing your cast and taking charge of your crew, I'm not even 20 years old and I am still learning myself about directing, so I'm in no position to give out advice. I'll leave all that to Lloyd, since this is his fucking book.

YOU'RE ALMOST THERE!

Once you have established your crew, found your actors, and planned out a reasonable shooting schedule, you will want to begin the rehearsal process as soon as possible. In fact, as I have previously stated (but will re-state so I can get to 322 pages . . .), you should break out a video camera and tape every single rehearsal as if you were already shooting the film. This will allow you to experiment with different shots and angles, while your actors work at memorizing their lines and developing their performances. This may sound like a giant pain in the ass, but it will help you tremendously when it comes time to actually shoot the movie.

In an ideal world, your cast and key crew will be working together in perfect harmony by the time actual shooting begins. This is the plan, anyway. With any luck your actors will have developed a keen awareness of who their characters are, and will have begun to add parts of their own personalities into their portrayals. Be open to any suggestions your actors may have regarding their roles.

For example, Jason Yachanin, the wonderful young actor who portrayed Arbie in *Poultrygeist*, decided that it would be great to have Arbie become even dumber and dumber than we had written as the film progressed. This is in stark contrast to most films, which tend to have their lead characters become more self-aware and capable over the course of the film. I thought that this was a

FIGURE 6.5 *Last known picture of Jim Henson with the Muppets.*

great idea. I don't think that he would have had the idea to make this decision if he didn't have adequate rehearsal time to develop and inhabit the character he was playing. As director, it is your job to remain open to such suggestions and improvisations.

YOU'RE GETTING EVEN CLOSER NOW!

When the time to start shooting on the actual sets and locations draws near, you should take all of your key crew to each and every location so that they can become familiar with the upcoming work environment. Make sure that they all know how to get to each location, and encourage them to show up to as many rehearsals as possible. After your actors have gotten comfortable with their lines, start shooting the rehearsals in full costume. You need to make sure that they can move around comfortably and perform the same actions in their costumes so that you don't wind up wasting time when you realize your lead actress can't dance as easily in combat boots as she did in sneakers during the rehearsals.

WAIT FOR IT . . . WAIT FOR IT . . .

If you have been following this book step by step so far, you will have developed an excellent script to work from, put together an eager and talented group of individuals to help you bring your vision to life, and rehearsed over and over again until you could shoot the entire movie in your sleep. Well, love, you better hold onto your body pillow. This is where the ride gets rough.

AND NOW . . .

It's time to start shooting!*

---

*UNDERAPPRECIATED FOOTNOTE GUY SAYS: You forgot about me, didn't you? You pieces of shit! Who did you think typed out those 20 footnotes? I bet you didn't think about it, did you . . . Jesus, sometimes I wish I had gone into another line of work.

Chapter seven

Managing the Set, or Mastering the Age-Old Art of Babysitting

Sometimes the F train between Long Island City and Lexington Avenue likes to fuck me over. Don't get me wrong. I'm not bitter about it. After 35 years at Troma, I've come to accept that life is a series of disappointments. Sad, sad disappointments. Waiting 40 minutes at the 21st Street subway station doesn't come close to my definition of true suffering.[1] Speaking of suffering, remind me to talk about *The Diving Bell and the Butterfly*. But not now.

When the F train does finally arrive to carry me away from Tromaville and back to Manhattan, I fully expect to emerge from underground with the frustrations of the day behind me. Who cares if *The New York Times* refuses to give *Poultrygeist: Night of the Chicken Dead* a decent-sized review, and instead relegates it to a small paragraph that no one will see? What does it matter if giant

---

[1]Anyone who sat through *27 Dresses* would certainly agree.

media conglomerates are taking over the world? I'm certainly not going to worry about it. The sun is setting over the power plant, and I'm ready to go home and kiss my wife.[2] When I get above ground, however, instead of my quiet, serene, tree-lined street, I'm confronted by some sort of high-security demilitarized zone. Helicopters hover in the air, and Brett Ratner himself might as well be sitting on a crane directing the whole thing.

Except he's not, and this is very, very real.

"Fuck, Kaufman. What did you do?"

Just then, I'm stopped dead in my tracks by a large police officer holding a machine gun and dressed in full combat gear. Over his incredible Hulk-like shoulder, concrete barricades zigzag across the streets, and rooftop snipers sit perched atop every building on my block. I'm a moment away from pissing myself when it all comes back to me — tomorrow just so happens to be the day that the Pope is bestowing his holy presence on New York City. A visit that will include conducting mass at the Catholic church across the street from my house.

Great. As if I didn't have enough shit to deal with.

After explaining to the He-Man cop that I actually live on this street, I begin to maneuver my way through the maze of concrete structures and barbed wire laid out in front of me. Part of my brain is picturing me stepping on a landmine, losing a leg, and ending up on *Dancing With the Stars* like Paul McCartney's ex.* Meanwhile, another part of me stares in amazement at the careful preparations that must have gone into the planning and execution of an event of this magnitude. The snipers on the roof are almost like the grips on a film set. The machine-gun toting cops are like PAs. And the Pope? He's like an actor person. All of these people had to work together as one unit to make this production happen. A movie set is kind of like this, only much, much more important.

Come to think of it, I have always thought that the Pope and I had a lot in common. After all, I am a self-hating Jew, while the Pope was a card-carrying Nazi youth. Not to mention the fact that

---

[2]By "kiss" I, of course, mean screw. And by "my wife," I, of course, mean my beard.

*EDITOR'S NOTE: Heather Mills McCartney didn't step on a landmine, Lloyd.

LLOYD'S RESPONSE: I never said she stepped on a landmine. I said she was on *Dancing With the Stars*, which I think might be worse.

both of us are involved with organizations that have a history of sex with young men.[3]

THE THREE RULES OF PRODUCTION

As soon as people set foot on your set, they should immediately be accosted by a sign reading the following:

1. Safety to humans.
2. Safety to other people's property.
3. Make a good movie (in much smaller type).

These rules should be posted everywhere — where the coffee is, in the porta-potties, everywhere! It's sort of what Chairman Mao did in China. (Thanks for that classy education, Yale!) By using slogans and colorful posters you can pretty much brainwash your cast and crew into running a safe production.[4] If you watch *Terror Firmer*, you will see these rules posted throughout the set of the movie-within-a-movie in the film. This is actually done on every Troma production. Post the rules of production everywhere, then when someone on your team inevitably fucks something up, you can scream at them for not being able to read, among other things. These three rules are of particular importance when you are shooting on location, especially when it is somebody else's property. It's similar to sexual intercourse — you don't want to piss off your host before you can even get a shot off.*

FIRST DAY JITTERS

When shooting begins, I never allow myself to be the first person to arrive on set. This might sound odd, considering that up to this point

---

[3]I often spend my Thursday nights giving lap dances at the Manhole Club, while the Pope has been a Catholic all of his life.

[4]These signs weren't posted on the set of an unnamed film shot in Tennessee where Troma's good friend and legendary scream queen Debbie Rochon nearly had her right hand severed by a machete. Personally, I don't know what I would do without my right hand . . .

*FOOTNOTE GUY SAYS: I'm sorry about my outburst earlier. If I had someone to talk to, I think everything would be okay. If anyone is on Google chat, my screen name is smallprintluver. Find me!

I've been involved in every painstaking detail of preproduction — from what type of food will be served to the quality of toilet paper to be used. Instead, I let the cast and crew arrive on set first so that they can get busy organizing all the decisions that I've already made. This isn't just a power trip. By this stage of the game, I feel confident that my cast and crew are more than capable of getting our shooting day up and running. Also, it's kind of a power trip.

This laissez-faire attitude is in stark contrast to how I behaved during the production of *Squeeze Play!*[5] Every day I was the first one on set, dealing with every aspect of the day's shoot. I wanted to be the guy to tell the caterer where to set up the food, where the trucks should be parked, where my hairless teenage boys were to be delivered — basically all of the normal aspects of a feature-film production. Apparently, I felt that the entire movie would self-destruct if I weren't there to constantly deal with every mundane detail in person. I was wrong.

I realized around the time of making *Sgt. Kabukiman, NYPD* (1990)[6] that I should stay the hell out of the nuts and bolts of daily preparation. After all, my not being there doesn't mean that the entire production will fall to pieces. In fact, my not showing up at all would probably guarantee a level of box office success never before known to a Troma film. What I finally realized is that, by showing up later, I wouldn't burn myself out on all of the inherent bullshit of setting up for a day of filming.

Instead, I use the precious morning hours to be creative and re-write scenes rather than worry over whether the coffee is ready (it's not) and the bagels are fresh (they aren't). So far this system has worked out extremely well for me, especially since I feel that morning hours are when I'm at my most creative. Also, if you're on a tight budget, you can usually find better deals on transvestite prostitutes early in the morning.

---

[5] *Squeeze Play!*, which I directed in 1976, was a satire about the Women's Liberation Movement, using a Gyno-American softball team as a metaphor. *The New York Times* called it "zesty!"

[6] This Oscar-winning movie is so well-known and beloved that there is really no need to describe it as I did with *Squeeze Play!**

*EDITOR'S NOTE: I watched *Sgt. Kabukiman, NYPD* when we were discussing this book deal, and I must agree . . . There is no need to describe it, because it stinks.

FOOTNOTE GUY SAYS: Wow, she's harsh!

When I finally get the call to arrive on set, I'm all revved up and dripping wet with artistic juices.[7] By steering clear of certain stressful situations, I guarantee that I'm all about creativity and artistic integrity from this point on in the day. My loyal cast and crew are more than capable of dealing with all the little bullshit details.

WHAT WE HAVE HERE IS A FAILURE TO COMMUNICATE

At the beginning of filming, it's important to establish and maintain a strict hierarchy of communication on your set. Every member of the cast and crew should voice any suggestions or concerns to their department heads, who will in turn tell your AD, who will then bring such things to your attention if it's something they can't take care of themselves. This might seem unnecessarily formal in the context of the film set "family," but trust me. When you're busy both directing a film and dealing with every asshole on set shouting ideas in your general direction, you'll understand. That being said, this isn't to say you shouldn't be open to ideas and suggestions from your cast and crew. In fact, it's quite the opposite. If you're making a comedy, I think you should encourage everyone on set to offer suggestions. After all, a good joke can come from anyone — from the lowliest PA to the guy delivering the pizza. Just make sure that all ideas are filtered through your system of communication and not just shouted out to you. This saves people from getting embarrassed should you shoot down their idea in front of the entire set, and allows you to take full credit for any brilliant ideas. You win both ways!

For example, in *Citizen Toxie* there is a gruesome shot where a car strikes a little old lady and the car's tires roll over her head. After we completed the shot, Brendan Flynt approached me and quietly offered up an idea.

"Hey Lloyd, why don't we take an old stunt mask and paint it up with blood and have a stunt double spin their eyes around so we can get a close-up?"

I thought this was a great idea. We bloodied up the mask, threw it on a stand-in double[8] lying on the ground and got the close-up of the woman's eyes spinning around.

---

[7]Yep, that's what those juices are.

[8]The double also doubled as the beautifully endowed naked sign language interpreter on screen, and tripled as the script supervisor off screen.

Then the line producer Patrick Cassidy came over to me and whispered in my other ear.

"Why don't you have her piss and shit herself too?"

We whipped up some fake excrement (at least I think it was fake . . . Patrick seemed a little too anxious to go get it for us) and we set up the shot. I had a special effects production assistant run a hose down the double's legs and directed her to kick her legs wildly as the piss and shit spilled from her beautifully thrashing body. Just thinking about it still brings a tear to my eye.

Sure, the whole thing probably cost us an extra hour or two, but it was worth it. In fact, this scene gets one of the biggest laughs of the entire film. So encourage people to offer ideas, but have them do it quietly. Sometimes they will be stupid ideas. Enthusiastic and well-intentioned, but stupid nonetheless.

ELI ROTH SAYS . . . (IT'S ALL YOUR FAULT)

David Lynch once told me "the only thing that matters — the only thing — is the information that is recorded in front of that frame." Nobody cares about the behind-the-scenes bullshit. Nobody cares if this person was fucking that person, or this person got a bigger trailer . . . nobody gives a shit. It's not going to wind up on camera. And it is your job as the director to make sure you get your shots . . . it is nobody else's fault. You can say, "This actor threw a fit and didn't want to come out of makeup because they were crying because this actor told them to fuck off and they fucked that person the day before . . ." Too bad; it's your fault. You put this whole thing together, it rests on your shoulders, and you better fucking fix it. So you're like "but I'm an artist!" Well, too bad. It is completely your fault. It is YOUR fault. It is YOUR responsibility. You have to take responsibility for everything as a director. And if you cast a certain actor and that actor is fucking crazy, you better figure out a way to get your scene and get them to calm down. There was an actor in Cabin Fever that was driving me crazy and I wanted to scream and I wanted to choke this person, but I bit my tongue and we got the scene and the scene played great. Everybody loved it. On Hostel I was really, really nice for the first two weeks of shooting and the crew started to think "Well, Eli's not like a real direc-tor. He's our friend; he's cool!" And then they all went out and got fucked up Sunday night and on Monday morning everybody was dragging ass and I went fucking crazy. I fired people and I threw people off set and those motherfuckers snapped to. You have to be an army general. That's directing.

FIGURE 7.1 Eli Roth, covered in blood after beating up some Crips, but still able to kick your ass.

STOMPING ON EGGSHELLS

Speaking of enthusiastic, well-intentioned, and occasionally stupid, I believe it was Alfred Hitchcock (or maybe Ricky Martin . . . I get the two of them confused) who famously said, "all actors are cattle." Very few of them actually enjoy the burning sensation of being branded, however. If all actors are cattle, then you as director are the cowboy, and it's your job to tend to your herd. Once you have assembled your final cast and crew, you'll find that a lot of your time will be spent acting as a babysitter and wet nurse rather than directing your movie.

An actor's ego is a fragile thing. For all of their onscreen bravado, most actors are incredibly neurotic and have absolutely zero self-confidence. They worry about their looks, their performance, whether anybody likes them, the sores on their nether regions — you name it. Perhaps that is why they have chosen to become actors in the first place — they can be somebody else for a while. After all, they have chosen a career in which they can pretend to be somebody who is more attractive, smarter, and cooler than they see themselves. Or maybe acting just really appeals to social retards. Hell, I've acted in about a hundred films! At any rate, it will be your duty to massage your actors' egos, providing them with the reassurance that they are, indeed, doing a mediocre job.

A LONG ISLAND CITY INTERLUDE

A few weeks ago, as I was walking one of my interns around the Troma Building's new Long Island City neighborhood, I happened upon a sign, written in black marker on a piece of rotting plywood, politely requesting that people not let their dogs shit on the front lawn of a building. I was taken aback. Dog shit is usually a subject that moves normally sane folks beyond politeness and into downright hostility. In this way, dog shit is kind of like directing. Take a compassionate and reasonable man such as myself, put him in a position where he is dealing with divas and deadbeats all day, every day, and you often end up with a steaming pile of dog shit in a bowtie. So let's take a lesson from this plywood sign. I was so impressed by its calm and beautiful tone that, out of respect, I didn't allow my intern[9] to shit on the lawn. A little finesse can go a long way.

ELI ROTH SAYS . . . (SAY THANK YOU)

Let me tell you something: the words "thank you" coming out of the mouth of the director will save your shoot. I remember working on some movies and the director was screaming and screaming and for the first five minutes everyone was tense, and after a while they were like "fuck you, dude" and they'll actually work slower to piss the director off. On the other hand, director Don Scardino couldn't have been nicer, and it was always an eight or nine hour day because everybody did their jobs because we all liked him. He said

---

[9]That intern was Lance Bass . . . or my future assistant Sara. I can't remember.*

*A NOTE FROM SARA: It was me, Lloyd. You were asking me if I wanted to write this book with you, and telling me what a shitty experience it would be.

  LLOYD'S RESPONSE: That's right! That was also the day I saw that heads-up penny in the filthy gutter water and superstitiously made Sara pick it up. But I let her keep it!

"hey, how's it going?" and "don't worry about it," and he said "thank you." Thank people for doing a good job, because at the end of the day, as much as people really want to make money in this business, people just really want to be appreciated. They just want to know that their work made a difference and what they did counted and mattered. So say "thanks" if someone did a great job. Say "Hey, great work guys. See you tomorrow!" Say "good morning" to your crew. A lot of directors I know have this air of aloofness, but once you've been a production assistant, and you've been at the bottom of the ladder, you know how it feels to be treated that way. You know what it's like to work for a director who treats you like shit, and you know how much harder you work for a director who is nice to you. And when the director says, "Hey, thank you! I know that sucked, but you really helped me out in a pinch," it makes a huge difference. These are all things that cost you no money, but will save your shoot.

ACTING OUT[10]

It's up to you to figure out how to coax the performances you need from your actors while serving as both counselor and therapist. How you go about doing this is entirely your call. Personally, I usually manage to guilt my actors into delivering the performances I need by breaking down crying and going on about what a failure I have become as a director. They usually feel sorry for me and put aside their own problems long enough to get their arms ripped off by a gigantic penis monster. Either that or I threaten to blow my brains out. If neither of these work, I play the part of an alcoholic father, who loves you when he's sober, and beats your brains out when he's tipsy. Not knowing what to expect keeps them on edge, and edgy people will usually do anything to please you. Like it or not, dealing with the easily bruised egos of your actors will be a big part of your production. The important thing to remember is that they are all human beings, and everyone on your set deserves to be respected as such.[11]

---

[10] *Acting Out* is now available on DVD from http://www.troma.com. BUY TROMA!*

   *EDITOR'S NOTE: Stop it, Lloyd.

[11] Or so I've been told. I'm still up in the air on this point.

FIGURE 7.2 *Special FX director Tom Devlin, Assistant Cameraman Arsenio Assin, and nuclear physicist Lloyd Kaufman rejoice while discovering penicillin back in 1932.*

SPEAKING OF RESPECT . . .

While shooting *Citizen Toxie*, our actor playing the Toxic Avenger, Dave Mattey,[12] came down with a bit of a diva complex. He would argue with me over certain shots and complain about the lousy working conditions. I could understand where he was coming from, but at the same time, we were trying to make a fucking movie. One day Dave decided to show up to the set a few hours late — a day when we happened to have a large number of actor persons for a huge crowd scene. Each day it would take about 3–4 hours to get Dave into his Toxie makeup, so time was of the essence. I did what any reasonable director would do in that situation — I immediately picked a short black guy off the street to fill in for Toxie in that scene. I had my people get him into costume and throw on a Toxie stunt mask. It looked good enough to me. I started to roll film.

Needless to say, when the 6'5" and very white Dave Mattey finally walked out onto the set to discover that a 5'10" black man in a crappy

---

[12]As Toxie, Dave once literally shoved someone's head up their ass. In an ironic twist, Dave appears in the Will Smith flick, *Hancock*, where his head is shoved up someone else's ass. I feel it's the best scene in *Hancock*.

FIGURE 7.3 *Time is of the essence, so Lloyd Kaufman devises a unique way to film and defecate at the same time.*

stunt mask had replaced him, he was more than a little pissed off. You see, for all of his delusions of stardom, Dave forgot one simple thing: he was a guy in a mask. And guys in masks can be switched out pretty easily. This is something that you as director can point out to your actors should a similar situation arise on your set. After a long, calm conversation between Dave and me regarding the matter (which included various uses of the terms "asshole" and "motherfucker"), we managed to come to a professional understanding. If I recall correctly, Dave was never late to the set again after that day. The lesson that you can take from all of this? Make a movie that includes lots of masks. In fact, when it came time to film *Poultrygeist: Night of the Chicken Dead*, I asked my lead actors Jason Yachanin and Kate Graham to wear masks in case I had to fire them. In fact one of the last shots of Kate is actually a 5′10″ black guy in a mask. Oh, the beauty of filmmaking! But let's talk about nudity . . . again!

A LITTLE NUDITY FOR THE ROAD

When you do shoot any scenes involving sex and nudity, be sure to respect your actor's privacy by maintaining a closed set during these scenes. Only the essential cast and crew should be present, and you should appoint someone to make sure that nobody "accidently" wanders onto the set. This was an ongoing problem during the production of *Citizen Toxie*, as half the fucking town seemed to pop out of nowhere and congregate on the set whenever a tit popped out of a blouse. Keeping a level of professionalism will do wonders to keep your actors from flaking out on you. Of course, on *Citizen Toxie*, my actress did, in fact, flake out on me.

AN AVERAGE DAY IN TROMAVILLE (WHEN EVERYTHING GOES ACCORDING TO PLAN, WHICH IS IN NO WAY AN "AVERAGE" OCCURENCE IN TROMAVILLE)

Let's take a look at what an average shooting day on a Troma set looks like when everything goes according to plan:

1. Trucks are parked so they can't possibly be "in the picture."
2. The coffee and "food" are set up.
3. Actors rehearse while the crew prepares.
4. We block the first scene with all department heads watching.
5. All necessary props are prepared and put in place.
6. Final art direction is set up.
7. Lights are placed into general position. We know which direction we're shooting in, as it has been discussed the night before.
8. The actors see blocking and go get dressed and into makeup.
9. DP and crew put lighting where it needs to be.
10. While actors are getting dressed, the DP and director can utilize stand-ins and perform technical rehearsals. This is when dolly shots, focus pulls, FX, and stunts will be run through.
11. Actors return in costumes and makeup.
12. Run a couple of rehearsals with everything in place.
13. Roll camera!
14. Lipstick-painted pigs fly, because nothing will ever go this smoothly. But at least you have something to aim for.

As director, you have to deal with the fact that you can't always get what you want. You need to balance getting your movie shot with achieving cinematic perfection. If too much time is wasted on one particular shot, you need to make the call and decide that "good enough" will have to do. This is especially true on the first day of shooting. If you fall behind on your first day you'll set a horrible, irreparable precedent for the rest of your shoot. In fact, you may damage your crew's perception of your leadership abilities, and everything will quickly turn to shit soon after that.[13]

You can't afford to burn time while you allow your DP to get the lighting perfect or your make-up artists to fix every last detail. There is plenty of time in between takes for your DP and make-up artists to continue perfecting their work. It's doubtful you'll get what you need on the first take anyway, and even if you do, you still need to shoot the coverage. Even with this mindset, it's always possible to get hung up on achieving a particular look. In times like these, a solid AD will step in and give you and your technical crew a swift kick in the ass, keeping things from really starting to drag.

LESSONS FROM A FIRST-TIME FEMALE DIRECTOR

Jenna Fischer stars on the mega-hit television comedy, The Office. *Lloyd met her before she got too famous and started making movies with Will Ferrell. Otherwise, she probably wouldn't have given him the time of day. Her amazing directorial debut film,* LolliLove, *is available from http://www.troma.com. BUY TROMA!*

When you're a first-time director, or a first-time filmmaker, allow yourself to make mistakes. Allow yourself to grab locations when you don't have a permit, allow yourself to have a plane fly through the middle of your audio. Just don't take yourself too seriously and have fun with it.

As a first-time director, you can also get a lot of stuff for free! When you're making your own movie people want to help you out. I had a girlfriend of mine get thousands of dollars by writing cards around Christmas time — when people like to give away money. She wrote this really sappy sort of Hallmark type letter all about how her dream, ever since she was a little girl, was to direct her own film, and that now she had written a film and all she needed was a little bit of money to get it made. And if people could dig into their pockets for $5 or $10, it would help make her dream come true and that she couldn't wait to then share the movie with all of these people. All these people mailed her checks for $20, for $100, for $150. She told them all, "don't give me a gift this year, just support my film and support me." It worked, and it was a great, great move!

---

[13] Just kidding. It will turn to shit anyway. God, are you discouraged yet? Because I sure am.

FIGURE 7.4 Jenna Fischer, star of *The Office*, receives the The TromaDance Film Festival's "Soul of Independence" award for her film *LolliLove*, while Lloyd Kaufman receives the "sole of Stephen Blackehart's shoe" award . . . hence the black eye.

With my film *LolliLove*, we had to do the movie based mostly on favors from people, so we were getting people for free. We weren't able to always be very selective. For example, our first editor was a very talented editor in reality television and he offered to edit our film for free. But we didn't end up having the same comedic sensibility. We tried to kind of overlook that for a while because he was offering his services. So we let him take a pass at the film and we really worked with him for a long time, but in the end we just had to bite the bullet and hire someone and pay them, because we couldn't get for free what we needed.

When it comes to directing, honestly, I think what I've learned above all is that I don't want to do it again! It was not the greatest experience of being a director. I enjoyed producing very much and I enjoyed acting in the film. But the directing aspect just really didn't light me up how I might have expected.

Sorry Lloyd . . .

HANGING OUT WITH THE TWINS

Going back to dragging, there was one particular incident during the filming of *Poultrygeist* that doesn't really apply to directing, but that I have a weird compulsion to talk about. During the scene where the young Arbie and Old Arbie, played by yours truly, sing and dance together, my testicles fell out of my thong without my knowing it. Brendan Flynt, my trusted Director of Photography, kept telling me "Lloyd, the twins[14] are out." I, of course, am not hep[15] to such lingo, so I just kept dancing happily along. Finally, a member of the crew took pity on me and told me that my balls were flapping around for all to see. I lost it. I literally could not stop laughing, no matter how hard I tried.

This was after hours and hours of shot after brutal shot, and I was no match for the delirium caused by my frazzled state. As a result, my dancing partner Jason Yachanin also burst into laughter. At the call of action, with very expensive 35mm film rolling, we would both collapse into fits of giggles like a couple of schoolgirls. Then we made love, right there in front of everyone. It was beautiful.

All right, so that part didn't happen. But for some strange reason, our soundman came over and slapped Jason as hard as he could across the face. Apparently, this was supposed to stop us from laughing. Instead, Jason almost quit.[16] What the soundman should have done was slap me. I don't really know if there's a point to this particular story, other than I couldn't resist the temptation to burn the mental image of an old Jewish man's wrinkly nut sack firmly into your frontal lobe. Actually, I guess the point is that whenever someone on your set gets out of line by doing something violent, fire them immediately.

Jason was understandably furious, demanded time off, and insisted on an airplane ticket. He left Buffalo,[17] where we were filming, which, of course, left my co-writer Gabe Friedman and I shitting ourselves in desperation, praying that Jason would find it in his heart to come back and finish the film with us. To his credit, he not only graciously returned, but he continued to give an excellent performance.

Speaking of needless violence, DP Brendan Flynt had made a habit of constantly ragging on our Gaffer, a kid named Yoshi. One day I was on the set minding my own business when I saw Yoshi violently charge Brendan in a blind rage. Before I knew it, Yoshi was on top of Brendan — beating the shit out of him. Suddenly we were

---

[14]I actually believed that by "the twins are out" Brendan was referring to Sirius A and Sirius B, the famous binary twin stars.

[15]I think the truly hep folks actually say "hip" instead of "hep."

[16]That certainly made me stop laughing! If Jason had quit, I might have had to dig my Jason Yachanin mask out of my trunk and play the role myself!

[17]Luckily, he went to Cleveland, which apparently was worse than being in Buffalo.

back in grade school and the entire crew surrounded the two as they tussled around on the ground, every single one of them cheering on Yoshi. Luckily, a couple of our guys, Beast and Steven, stepped in and stopped the fight before my erection became too noticeable. I sent Yoshi packing,[18] but it was kind of neat to watch Brendan get handled like that.[19]

I guess that story was even more pointless than the one about my balls hanging out, but doesn't it kind of make you giggle to think about a Director of Photography getting attacked by someone named Yoshi?*

WHAT NOT TO DO IN A NUTSHELL

While I certainly appreciate the raw energy and enthusiasm of young independent filmmakers, I often witness the same mistakes being made over and over again while on their sets. This perplexes me, since every single one of these young artists swears that they have read my books and watched my documentaries. I would like to think if this were true, they wouldn't be making the same fucking mistakes[20] I constantly warn them against.

David Silvio, the director of *Meat For Satan's Icebox*, was full of artistic exuberance and ideas that pushed the limits of Grand Guignol horror cinema. Unfortunately, he neglected to use a boom mic. Instead, the entire movie was shot using the omni-directional mic located inside of the video camera that his crew was shooting with. An omni-directional mic means that every single sound, from the dialogue coming from the actor's mouth to the guy taking a shit two rooms over, will show up on tape.

If you neglect to use a proper directional boom mic, all of that overlapping Altmanesque dialogue you spent hours crafting won't add up to a hill of navy beans because no one will be able to hear it.

---

[18]Why didn't I fire Brendan for antagonizing poor Yoshi? I already explained that I had worked with Brendan on several films and that breaking in a new DP would have been a pain in the ass. Also, Brendan owned all the camera equipment. Life ain't always fair, kids.

[19]I've been informed by some of the Troma Team that this incident was much milder than I have described it here, but I maintain that there was an all-out brawl.

*EDITOR'S NOTE: Lloyd, where are the pearls of wisdom about directing? You said this book would be inspiring. I'm not feeling inspired to do anything except cancel this book deal . . .

[20]And by mistakes, I mean choosing to be a low-budget independent filmmaker for 40 fucking years.

FIGURE 7.5 *Even when the acne gets really bad, a good director never gives up.*

Silvio also paid no attention to lighting. Instead, the entire thing was lit with whatever light source each location had available. This isn't exactly what Stanley Cortez[21] referred to as "painting with lights."

Silvio also opted to shoot with two cameras. This poses a problem if no camera tests are done and the cameras aren't properly white balanced and corrected so that the two images are indistinguishable from each other. Instead of seamlessly cutting together footage from the wide variety of available coverage, *Meat For Satan's Icebox* looks like it was shot with two different cameras. To top

---

[21]Cortez was a noted cinematographer who lit such films as *All About Eve* and Sam Fuller's *Shock Corridor*. His father was a noted Spanish explorer in Mexico who exterminated the Aztec race in 1522.

Bennys autograph of Lloyd

FIGURE 7.6 *Lloyd Kaufman burps after accidentally swallowing a Sharpie Permanent Marker.*

things off, actual animal parts were used for all the special effects, creating an onset biohazard for everyone involved.

Ultimately, despite having a great idea, *Meat For Satan's Icebox* is rife with problems. The film had everything going for it — blood, nudity, bondage, and a cameo by yours truly drinking urine.[22] But none of these things could make up for the lack of proper sound and lighting. If not for the technical ineptitude, the film could have been another *Bloodsucking Freaks*. But while *Bloodsucking Freaks* was made back in 1974 for very little money, it was still technically proficient. Shot on 35 mm, *Bloodsucking Freaks* was well-lit and actually looks like a real film. All the perversion, misogyny, sadism, dwarfism, and penis-eating lesbo-cannibalism almost take on a film noir, art house feel.

Thanks to the digital revolution, anyone with an idea and a group of willing accomplices can churn out a feature-length film in a few weeks. Unfortunately, many of these overzealous folks are doing so without bothering to learn even the most basic conventions of filmmaking. Don't get me wrong here; we have all made mistakes

---

[22]Which in itself isn't unusual, but it is rarely caught on film.

while making our movies, and indeed, you learn by doing. It's when you keep making the same mistakes over and over again that you have a serious problem. The fact of the matter is, technical ineptitude will pose a serious problem when seeking distribution for your movie. The people who are distributing DVDs for a living will be far less forgiving of your poor lighting and sound than your friends will.

Basically, only an absolute retard would actually pump the money needed into the manufacturing, marketing, and shipping of such a movie. Fortunately for the guys behind *Meat For Satan's Icebox*, such retards actually do exist. I am proud to say that Troma picked up *Meat For Satan's Icebox* for distribution.[23] Hopefully David Silvio and his team have learned from their mistakes and will produce a higher quality film next time out — a film so good that they won't even consider giving it to Troma for distribution!

SPEAKING OF MANAGEMENT

Sara, my dutiful assistant and co-writer, walks into my office, chewing on a pen. She sits.

"Did you see that e-mail you got from Elinor?"

I hadn't checked my e-mails yet, as it was only noon and I had only been in the office for a few minutes.

"I don't think so. What it is? She liked the last chapter?"

The pen is getting chewed to bits at this point.

"She says that the book isn't long enough. She says that your contract says 322 pages, and we're not even close. Did you know it had to be that long?"

"I think it's written somewhere." I move a Toxic Crusaders action figure on my desk, trying to find the literary contract. Sara watches me for a moment.

"All the sidebars are written. I've called everyone in your address book for an interview. No one will return my calls. I don't know what else to do."

"I wouldn't worry about it . . ."

"She says if it's not long enough, you won't get paid."

"Oh shit."

---

[23] *Meat for Satan's Icebox* is available for purchase in the Zombies vs. Satan Double Feature DVD from http://www.troma.com. BUY TROMA!

We sit in silence for a moment.

"Don't we have any more of that Eli Roth interview? That was pretty long, right?"

She nods, and gets up from the chair.

"We should write something about music videos, too. That will take up some space. And be informative. . ."

She has already escaped back to her desk, and I'm not sure if she heard me.

ELI ROTH SAYS . . . (ACTUAL DIRECTING IS . . .)

I went to film school, but the best experience I got for making a film was the three years I spent as a camp counselor for a group of thirty-five ten-to-eleven year-old boys, and I had to manage all of them and I had to keep them calm and had to keep them from fighting. That is your job as a director.

The truth is that when you're making a film — when you're actually shooting the film — there is very little directing involved. It's time management and babysitting — a whole different set of skills. When you're rehearsing, when you're working with your actors, that's when you're directing. In preproduction, when you sit down and talk with your DP, and talk through every scene, that's when you're directing. When you're actually shooting the movie, it's like "Oh, fuck, we have four hours to get this scene and we have thirty-six shots to do!" You better have your shot list, and the actors have to know what's going on. And that's all stuff you do in preproduction, because when you're actually shooting the film, it's very, very expensive. Even if you have a small crew of seven or eight people, that's seven or eight people that you have to feed.

Your job as the director is to communicate to your crew effectively, quickly, and succinctly. Nobody cares that "this is going to be the greatest movie ever!" Once you're shooting, the lighting guy is thinking "do I move the generator there or there? Where do I stage my equipment?" And the sound guy is thinking "where do I put my sound cart?" That's all they think about.

STUART GORDON ON PLUMBING

Everyone wants to direct, and that's because everybody can direct. You know if you want to be a plumber you have to go to plumbing school. You have to become an apprentice plumber for several years until finally you're given your plumbing license and then you're able to become a plumber. What is the job of the director? Some people say that it is to interpret the script — to bring the script to the screen. Basically, to become a film director, you just have to have the opportunity to direct a film. And what it really comes down to, in my opinion, is making choices. Deciding whether you're going to do this script or that script, whether you're going to use this actor or that actor, whether you're going to put the camera over here or over there, whether the actress is going to wear a red dress or a blue dress, whether it's going to be a close-up or two-shot and so forth. It's a series of decisions and if the decisions that you make work and the movie turns out well then you are a director and you get to direct another movie. If they don't, then it's time to check out plumbing school.

MY EDITOR ALSO SAID THOSE STORIES ACTUALLY DO NEED TO HAVE A POINT OR I NEED TO TAKE THEM OUT, AND I CAN'T EXACTLY AFFORD TO LOSE ANY WORDS RIGHT NOW, SO . . .

I take it back — I've spent a lot of time thinking about this, and the stories about Jason and the sound guy and Yoshi and my testicles may actually have a point. You decide to be a director because you want to make a movie. If you wanted to be a babysitter, you would have put up a flyer and advertised yourself as a babysitter. But the reality is, by becoming a director, you are essentially becoming a babysitter. You aren't going to be sitting on a crane and telepathically communicating your artistic vision to the crew. You actually have to talk to people. You have to deal with people. You have to fucking kiss boo-boos and make them better. This isn't a bad thing. But be ready. Sound design and lighting and camera angles are all key issues for your movie being at all successful once it is made. But to actually get a movie made without it going to shit halfway through the shoot, you have to actually be able to manage your set. So put *Labyrinth* on pause, get out of your basement, and go practice talking to someone.*

---

*FOOTNOTE GUY SAYS: If anyone needs to talk, I'm available. I can talk dirty if you want.

Chapter eight

Putting the "Special" in Special Effects, or Why We Spend 80% of Our Budget on Bromo-Seltzer

It may seem strange to some people that a company with no money, making a low-budget film for no money, and paying its crew in cheese sandwiches, would choose to spend hundreds of dollars, nay — even thousands of dollars of its meager budget on special effects. Why not spend that money on turkey sandwiches or working equipment? The fact is, in a film without any big stars, the special effects are what people want to see. The audience isn't going to care if your sound guy was paid an extra $200, but they will care if you are able to rip someone's testicles off and deep-fry them in oil. Now, it's obvious that we can't compete with CGI effects sequences costing millions of dollars, so at Troma, we tend to lean toward the humorous, slapstick, and original. When we put the infamous head crush in *The Toxic Avenger*, it was revolutionary! Now, every film and television show you see, from *South Park* to *High School Musical XVII* to *The Today Show* has a head crushing scene in it. Go figure . . . I guarantee that 20 years from now, more[1] people will remember the toilet cam/explosive diarrhea scene in *Poultrygeist: Night of the Chicken Dead* than the best special effects in *Indian Jones 4: Skull Fucker*.

FIGURE 8.1 *Lloyd Kaufman during his Abu Ghraib days.*

A *POULTRYGEIST* INTERLUDE CIRCA AUGUST, 2005

I'm standing in the muggy confines of the old McDonald's that we have recently converted into the primary location, American Chicken Bunker, for our latest film, *Poultrygeist: Night of the Chicken Dead.* It's summer, and it's hot as hell. The Troma Team has swarmed upon

---

[1] Okay, maybe not *more* people. Probably around five people total. But definitely a larger *percentage* of people who saw both films.

Buffalo, New York, like a pack of malnourished, sex-starved locusts with a singular objective — get our movie made. The sweltering heat and confined space have mixed together to create an unholy aroma of feet, sweat, balls, and swamp ass, which permeates the heavy air. I don't know how we managed to make a McDonald's even more disgusting than when it's serving chemically altered "meat" in Big Mac form, but somehow we have. Shockingly, aside from the smell, things have gone surprisingly well on set. We are in the homestretch, but after eight weeks in Tromaville, the crew is getting restless.

"Lloyd," I hear from behind me. I turn to see Andy Deemer, a producer on the film, approaching. He looks concerned. This can't be good.

"Lloyd," he continues, "I think we have a problem." My heart starts to sink.

"What sort of problem?" I ask, shoving three Twizzlers into my mouth as a preventative measure to keep from screaming.

"It's the General Chicken monster," Andy replies. "It looks bad." Andy hangs his head in shame, trying to avoid making direct eye contact with me.

"What do you mean, bad?"

"I don't think you can even tell what it's supposed to be."

"Can you at least tell it's a bird?" I ask, getting nervous. Andy doesn't answer right away, which makes me even more nervous.

"Sort of . . ."

Andy calls over to someone in the next room, who emerges wearing what is supposed to be the big scary General Chicken costume for our big finale. I am less than pleased.

"GOD DAMMIT!" I scream, spitting the Twizzler ends dangerously close to Andy's shoes. "This isn't a Zombie General. It's a fucking Myna bird!"

"I'm sorry Lloyd," Andy continues. "The special effects guys have been working their asses off on other stuff."

"This is asshole time. This is supposed to be our big special effects finale, and it's going to look like shit! Where's Gabe?!"

Gabe Friedman, who has come up behind us during my tirade, quietly mumbles, "I told you so . . ."

Andy starts to sob uncontrollably. I calm down a little. The truth was, Gabe had been warning me all along that the General Chicken scene was in trouble, but I had blown him off. I hadn't followed my own advice and checked the costume and effects months ahead of time. At that point, I should have made the special effects crew stay up all night and fix it.

FIGURE 8.2 *Cowriter, Supervising Editor, and fast-food technician Gabe Friedman stands proudly with Lloyd Kaufman as Steven Spielbird visits the set of* Poultrygeist.

"Fuck it," I declare. "We need to get this shot. Maybe it will look better when we blow it up."

A MORE ACCURATE *POULTRYGEIST* INTERLUDE . . . BY ANDY DEEMER

Dear Readers,

After spending months in Buffalo before filming began recruiting an unpaid crew, coordinating auditions, massaging egos, testing special effects, and managing all of Lloyd's "friends" who dropped out of GED classes to come hang out on the set because Lloyd told them they could be PAs, I feel like I'm a little more qualified to discuss the special effects challenges of *Poultrygeist* than Uncle Lloyd, who spent the week before filming began on holiday in Cancun.

Also, I didn't sob uncontrollably. At least not in front of Lloyd. I did, however, keep a journal on the *Poultrygeist* set, just in case Lloyd ever tried to re-imagine what it was really like. See for yourself . . .

ANDY DEEMER'S PRODUCTION DIARIES

Friday, June 17, 2005

Budget Crisis

In *Poultrygeist*, there are many effects, and a couple of those effects involve small explosions.

1. Arbie and Old Arbie both shoot guns.
2. Bullets hit a couple of zombies.
3. We blow up a small miniature of the Chicken Bunker.

Drew G, the gun/pyro expert, got back to us with his estimate today . . . $10,000.

To give some perspective, that's a third of our special effects budget on two short scenes. A few shots, even. Probably half a minute of film at most. To give further perspective, that's 5% of the movie's budget on 30 seconds of the film. I immediately called Ray, the local (possibly Mafioso) amateur FX guy, who carries a short baseball bat in the front seat of his Cadillac, a gun in his glove compartment, dresses like a Don, and refuses to answer questions about what he does for a living. He's got some street smarts. He's promised to put together a $500 substitute.

posted at 12:13 p.m.

Effects Ladies

Another long day. And a crazy long week. The big bad news today was the discovery of why the box of zombie mutant eggs that Bitte (our Stockholm-based egg maker) had sent from Sweden hadn't shown up. It turns out that they were seized by U. S. Customs, and are somewhere in one of the 300+ entry point holding cells, awaiting examination and possible destruction.[2] Fricking mutant eggs. Fricking terrorists.

After getting out of work tonight at 10 p.m., I headed down to the tacky Chelsea Hotel to meet FX Lady-slash-Lemmy-groupie Leah to pick up prosthetics for *Poultrygeist*. Leah had warned me that she was working on a low-budget

---

[2] It is a little known fact that since 9/11 Homeland Security has banned the importation of mysterious, large, goofy, vein-covered eggs.

film, but as I wandered into room 306, my eyes were immediately drawn to the foreign-accented couple whispering on the bed, the empty bottle of Jack Daniels on the bedside table, and the half-naked black man sitting on the toilet, Leah applying latex to his face. All I could think was . . . well . . . zombie porn.

"What are you guys shooting?" I asked as Leah pulled me outside.

"Nothing . . . I'll tell you later." Yeah, right. It was shady as hell. Of course, when she reached into her purse and pulled out a bloody penis (for the scene in *Poultrygeist* where the Irish Priest finds a severed willy in his sandwich) and a dog tag chain of severed ears (for when Vietnam vet Denny remarks to Arbie, "Hey man — I like your bling! Check these out — I got mine in 'Nam!"), it felt all the more tawdry.

posted at 11:48 p.m.

From my outbox . . .

"Something else we'd like to have you guys tackle is the fried chicken with the zits on it (see scene 53). Can you cast some KFC, color it, and then make zits that pulsate (and perhaps pop and spew out zitty pus fluid?)"

posted at 4:09 p.m.

The Dude

Most of today was spent with the small Swedish FX girl Bitte; and the huge bearded mountain man of FX, David G. David, showed us his basement in a neighboring town, filled with molds of ripped-apart zombie faces, and his garage, which he'd converted into a chicken medieval dungeon. He made promise after promise of everything he could make for us — but every few offers, he'd suffix with a slow "Although I'm really blocked up until September, you know." (September being well after *Poultrygeist* will be in the can.) "Oh, the grinder, yeah. I got an idea for that. Real simple," he'd say. Or, "The graveyard? Oh, I can do that easily. . . . We can work that out in a few hours." He took us to his warehouse. Four floors of crazy industrial machines and old props from plays and movies he'd worked on. A mechanical dog. A poorly wallpapered wall, leaning by itself against a crate, and marked "kitchen." A jet airplane fan. And dozens of leaking oil drums.

"Who owns all this stuff?"

"Oh, you know, a bunch of guys." From looks to voice to mannerisms, he *is* The Dude.

"So, David, you keep saying you'll do all this shit for us, but then you also keep saying how busy you are. How are you going to make both the grinder that Paco falls into and the toilet where the demon chicken pulls Jared's guts out through his anus?"

"Well, you know, I'm real busy, but you know, everything's a little easier when you add some turkey."

"Huh?"

"You know, *turkey*."

FIGURE 8.3 President Palin's version of "a chicken in every pot." Please note that the arm in the lower left corner operating this puppet is not, in fact, Dick Cheney.

So much for getting this stuff for free. We did leave with a couple of the zombie face molds, a quarter-bucket of latex, and Bitte's scarred memory of David asking her repeatedly for her bra size. Oh, and the roof of the McDonald's is still leaking water inside at a violent rate.

posted at 10:22 p.m.

Thursday, June 23, 2005

Huge Amounts of Blood

I nervously called Lloyd with a shopping list of FX materials, a $1500 estimate. But instead of barking that I was wasting his money, his normal angry reaction, he demanded "That's not enough blood! How much blood is there? We need huge amounts of blood! And greasy slimy shit too! KY jelly — we need buckets of it! This should be the bloodiest movie in history!"

posted at 11:10 a.m.

KabukiCar

In the early 1990s, Lloyd invested a decent amount of cash into a scene for *Sgt Kabukiman, NYPD*, where a 1979 giant green Dodge flips into the air and then explodes. To make up for this investment, he's reused this footage for every film since. Some character always climbs into a green car, and you know that car will somehow flip and explode. Of course, *Poultrygeist* will reuse the same footage. However, I'm now faced with the same problems that every other Troma producer has come up against. 1979 Dodges are rare, and are getting rarer every year. Green was also the least popular color. On *Citizen Toxie*, the producers found a blue 1970s Buick, and used that. On *Terror Firmer*, they bought a broken down car from a junkyard, spray painted it green, and paid a mechanic to get it running for one block. I've sent PAs to junkyards, and had them calling mechanics, but no luck so far.

posted at 11:35 p.m.

Details

Lloyd is so obsessed with certain details, and so fueled by tics and paranoias, he has me following in his footsteps. A month ago, he freaked out when I didn't pick up a heads-up penny we saw on the pavement. I was trying to discuss the budget, and he started ranting about this penny. "You've got to pick it up! It's heads up! Pick the damn thing up!" Ever since, I've obsessively collected every heads-up penny I've passed. *Obsessively.*

posted at 8:52 p.m.

Blood

People will randomly walk into the office, drenched in blood. Earlier today FX beauty Bitte, and then AD Caleb. Caleb was literally dripping, smearing it across the poor church rectory[3] carpet.

posted at 4:06 p.m.

Meeting with Lloyd

"When they do shit, can we do it so they squirt in someone's face? But again — it's gotta be thicker! It looks too thin! It looks like milk!" He then spent two minutes acting out a chicken zombie shitting explosive shit, and the reaction of the victims.

posted at 6:11 p.m.

---

[3] We rented an empty church to use as a production office, living quarters, and place to build sets and create special effects and props. We also filmed a few steamy nude scenes at the church since the McDonald's contract forbade filming nudity.

KabukiCar, Part II

The KabukiCar was located, finally, on Thursday. Just in time to film on Saturday. It's being borrowed from some old lady whose only request was that we drive her around all day. Former PA Ben spent weeks looking for it — claiming he'd exhausted every avenue. The young woman we put in charge of the task managed to secure this car in 24 hours.

posted at 3:13 p.m.

Oppressive Negativity

As I get off the phone, I mention to FX assistant Melissa, "So they said they might do the head-being-crushed-in-the-grinder effect tonight — is the head here, or at the restaurant?"

"We can't do that!"

"Why?"

"Because it's fucked. It's completely fucked!!!"

"But I thought we had a good head"

"We have nothing. It's all fucked."

"But what about Tom's head? The scored one?" She's now on the brink of tears.

"That's not made of gelatin! The gelatin ones are all fucked! Everything is just fucked!!"

"We don't need gelatin — we just need a head. We can use Tom's — it looks good. But the gelatin ones, if they're in the right shape, they can work too."

"But they're all fucked. They can't be painted. They can't have hair on them. They're fucked. I told someone to turn on the dehumidifier, and it's not on, and they're going to be fucked."

"Can we turn on the dehumidifier? Where is it? I'll turn it on. They just have to be the right shape — so it looks like something is being ground up."

"Fuck! I can't . . . fuck . . . I'll do it. I can't fucking speak. It's . . . fuck, I'll just do it."

posted at 8:37 p.m.

Two Isolated Quotes from a meeting with Lloyd last night . . .

Lloyd: "We'll definitely rip open a vagina, and stuff shit in it. At least we'll do that."

and

Bitte: "So the last word on the puppet is it *is* fucking the ass?"

posted at 12:08 a.m.

Tuesday, August 09, 2005

FX Woes Pt. XXXIV

The woes with the FX department are never ending, it seems. On Saturday, we scheduled video tests of a bunch of effects, for Gabe and me to give approval. Everyone said they'd be ready by Monday at 2 p.m. At noon, they requested another hour, so we knocked the tests back to 3 p.m. At 4 p.m., they still weren't ready. At 5 p.m., they still weren't. Bitte did two tests — an eye being pecked out and baby zombie chicks hatching from egg-breasts. Both looked good, but both fell apart halfway through the test. Tom did one test — obese Jared shitting himself down to thin size. The effect was unpainted, missing hair, looked fake, and was scheduled to be filmed for real in 12 hours. He stayed up all night working on fixing it.

Chris and Xochitl were scheduled to do four tests. The first was a man having his face and chest shredded by zombie arms . . . it looked like they'd bought some crappy Halloween makeup at the mall and pasted it on. The second was a man having his ear ripped off . . . it looked like someone glued a potato to the side of his head, had no slime and almost no blood, and then a pump they were using exploded in the actor's face. The third test was me being scalped — they brought a bald head prosthetic that looked nothing like me, was painted blue, and was just completely unacceptable. The fourth test they didn't have ready. Finally, there's Dave and Melissa, who were scheduled for two tests. They didn't even show up. We called around until we found that they'd literally run away. Caleb got Dave on the phone, who was babbling near-incoherently about having to help his mother in Ohio move. Doug, who they were staying with, has also been not showing up, and when he does, looks ragged and wasted. I'm starting to worry that they might be doing meth or something else terrible. Anyhow, it was all a complete waste of time . . . so we're now working on how to have a huge zombie massacre take place this weekend — it might not be anywhere near as grand as planned.

posted at 12:37 p.m.

Thursday, August 11, 2005

Speed

Things moved at a snail's pace on set today . . . Lloyd got no sleep last night, and fell asleep repeatedly on set. He was also in a terrible mood. He called me up at noon, screaming about how FX needed to test The General Monster transformation today. It was already scheduled for 9 p.m. He screamed maniacally, "it has to be done sooner! What the fuck! They're doing nothing down there, Andy! They've had weeks, months, to work on this shit!" So I pulled it

> forward, and scheduled it for 6 p.m. He freaked out again. I rescheduled it for "ASAP." Of course, it looked like shit. He freaked out. Now it's 2:20 a.m. and we're freaking out, trying to get shit together for the huge massacre that's scheduled to start in two days, and that we have nothing for. Nothing.
>
> *posted at* 2:21 a.m.

Well, that's about it. My "special" special effects experience boils down to these three pieces of advice:

1. Don't hire fuckups.
2. Schedule all FX tests as early as possible, so that when they go to shit, there is time to fix them.
3. Don't go to Cancun the week before filming.[4]

Regards,
Andy

BACK TO LLOYD (WARNING: DON'T EVER ACTUALLY TURN YOUR BACK TO LLOYD)

Luckily for me, I always set aside a few days and extra money to go back and shoot any pick-up shots we might need to get after production. I knew the second I saw the General Chicken scene on playback that I would need to do it all over again. But if I had properly pre-planned and rehearsed this shot, I would have gotten it right the first time. Now, when you see the film, the General Chicken Monster looks slightly less like a Myna bird and the explosion looks a little bit better than your typical Fourth of July accident. However, had I taken the time to do proper dress rehearsals and film them, the above-mentioned disaster could have been avoided entirely, saving me the time and expense of going back and shooting it all over. But even if the shot in question comes across as underwhelming while you're shooting, keep the camera rolling. Perhaps there will be a few frames here and there that can be salvaged and used

---

[4] LLOYD'S RESPONSE: The weekend in Cancun was a business trip with our sales representatives. In case anyone was thinking that I had fun, the place was 98% fat old men and one cute lesbian. One of the reasons Troma is still in business is that I am willing to sacrifice my time and go to Cancun when the need arises. Unfortunately, my needs really had no reason to arise that weekend.

during the editing process to save the scene. I feel this is especially true during gore scenes. While your actors are being slaughtered, keep slathering on blood, tissue paper, and UltraSlime™ and the shot may turn out to be great after all!

FIGURE 8.4 *After the Russian skin peel.*

WHY NOT JUST USE CGI, YOU STUPID OLD MAN??

There are actually two instances in *Poultrygeist* where we used CGI effects. In one scene, we digitally erased two strings coming out of a man's exploding egg-breasts. Unfortunately, we left the strings in for two other shots. The other CGI effect is in the scene where a zombie is hit by a spray of beer and we needed to create a smoking wound. In my opinion, CGI always looks fake. Real special effects often look fake too, but they are a hell of a lot cheaper. Then again, I didn't grow up on video games, and those who did seem much more willing to accept the idea of CGI effects being somewhat realistic. Fucking kids . . .

TALKING SHIT

Earlier, I mentioned the toilet cam/explosive diarrhea scene in *Poultrygeist*. If you haven't seen the film, basically a very large man, played by Joe Fleishaker, ingests a suspiciously pulsating egg at American Chicken Bunker, sprays shit all over a bathroom stall, and then turns himself inside out, emerging from the shit-stained bathroom as a skinny, bloody, inside out zombie. For this sequence, we had to build a fake Joe Fleishaker ass and figure out how to shoot the Baby Ruth/chocolate pudding shit out of that fake ass. Joe wasn't in good health, and our not-quite-as-large pal Ron Mackey ended up doing most of the stunts. All together, we spent very little money on the scene, but a whole day of filming. My wife, as an executive producer, ended up censoring the view from inside the toilet, but this scene still gets one of the biggest audience reactions in the entire film. Bigger, I'm sure, then anything in *Indian Jones and the Curse of the Crystal Piece of Shit.*[5]

FIGURE 8.5 *The editors are still attempting to determine, between Lloyd Kaufman and this prosthetic butt, who, exactly, is the bigger ass.*

---

[5] However, this didn't stop *Poultrygeist* from getting kicked out of New York's Village East Cinema in its third week for *Indian Jones*. Sometimes life's a bitch, unless you're Steven Spielberg.

GETTING THE RIGHT FOLKS FOR THE JOB

When hiring a stunt coordinator and special effects coordinator, take the time to get the best person possible for each job. While it may be okay to hire your functionally retarded siblings to serve as PAs and costume designers,[6] your stunt and special effects coordinators aren't positions to be taken lightly. After all, these folks are responsible not only for the visual quality of your film, but for the safety of your cast and crew as well. The last thing you want is a mass re-enactment of Vic Morrow's *Twilight Zone* decapitation just because you were too lazy to find a quality stunt coordinator.

The stunt and special effects coordinators need to work in sync to prevent any on-set injuries while also delivering the best shots possible. This is one instance that I truly believe it is best to stay the hell out of the way and let your coordinators do their jobs. Especially if they happen to be highly regarded and experienced within their respective fields. Ideally they will work in tandem to ensure high quality and safety. Sure, the effects guys might want certain explosions to pack a little more punch, and you as director might be inclined to allow them to do so, but your stunt coordinator should have a say as well. Particularly if she[7] feels that placing your actors within two feet of explosive charges might not be such a great idea. If you ever feel that your stunt and effects coordinators aren't looking out for your actors' safety, get rid of them immediately. After all, car crashes, explosions, and stair falls are serious business, and the last thing you want is someone getting needlessly hurt on your watch.[8] Okay, well, the last thing you probably want is a butter and mayonnaise sandwich on rye, but someone getting hurt is a close second.

You should also check around ahead of time to see if there may be a safer or even cheaper way to pull off a certain special effect.

---

[6] Not that these jobs are any less important. But unlike special effects and stunts, these jobs don't usually have the potential to kill people.

[7] You'd forgotten about my gender-equalizing pronouns, hadn't you? Shame on you. For the record, everyone knows that all stunt coordinators, as well as U. S. presidents, are guys.*

*EDITOR'S RESPONSE: Jesus, Lloyd . . .

[8] This, of course, doesn't apply to snuff.

Professional FX folks love using squibs.[9] Unfortunately for the low-budget independent filmmaker, squibs are pretty expensive, and can eat up a large chunk of your budget. For *Poultrygeist*, we found a guy in Buffalo who owned several air guns. Using these air guns instead of exploding stuff on the actors was far less dangerous, much cheaper, and required little set up time. And with a little creative editing, I think seemed just as realistic.

LOVE THE STUNT? USE IT AGAIN! (AND AGAIN . . . AND AGAIN . . .)

It's no secret that the car flip we staged for *Sgt. Kabukiman, NYPD* has been recycled numerous times in our films. I do this for a couple of reasons:

1. The stunt came off incredibly well. So well, in fact, that I like to show it over and over again just to prove that I can shoot something so awesome.
2. The stunt cost a hell of a lot of cash, and I intend to milk every single penny I can out of it by repeatedly using it in my films.

Recently, I was at the Avignon Film Festival where they showed *Poultrygeist: Night of the Chicken Dead* to a full house. These were regular people, not your typical Troma fans, and didn't realize that the car flip at the end was a recycled stunt. They cheered when the car flipped and crashed, and loved the scene just as much as the folks in the sold-out New York City premiere, who recognized it. That's another reason why I continue to use the footage in every film. It works on its own as a cool fucking stunt, but is also a little wink to our fans.

If you do manage to carry out a particularly spectacular looking stunt or special effects shot, feel free to use it as many times as possible in your films. There is no shame there. This shit isn't cheap, and any added production value you can muster will only help you when it comes time to find a distributor.

---

[9]Small explosions with small blood bags used to simulate a bullet hitting a body.

Poultrygeist Hatching in Los Angeles, June 13th, 2008

"A VERITABLE CLUCKWORK ORANGE..." -VARIETY

"THE BEST FILM TROMA'S EVER PRODUCED, AND CERTAINLY LLOYD KAUFMAN'S MOST ACCOMPLISHED." -C.H.U.D.

A LLOYD KAUFMAN/MICHAEL HERZ PRODUCTION

POULTRYGEIST

NIGHT OF THE CHICKEN DEAD

OPENS JUNE 13TH AT THE LAEMMLE'S SUNSET 5
8000 SUNSET BLVD. WEST HOLLYWOOD. 90046 PH: 323.848.3500
ACCLAIMED DIRECTOR LLOYD KAUFMAN AND CAST APPEARING
IN PERSON JUNE 13TH!

FIGURE 8.6 *Paris Hilton in a rare early morning photograph.*

--------------------------Original Message--------------------------

From: elinor@repress.com
Sent: Aug 31, 2008 11:03 PM
To: Lloyd Kaufman <lloyd@troma.com >
Subject: RE: chapter 8

Lloyd,

Love the stuff from Andy! This is really the practical kind of experience that we were hoping to get from you. Can we get some more practical experience/advice in the next couple of chapters? Thanks!

Best,
Elinor

Sent via BlackBerry by AT&T

---------------------------End Message--------------------------------

MORE PRACTICAL DIRECTING TIPS, AS PER ELINOR'S INSISTENCE — "HOW TO SOUND LIKE A DIRECTOR"

The only thing more important than looking like a director is sounding like a director. Very few people on your set will be deaf, so sounding like a director is one of the easiest ways to earn instant street cred.

1. Yell "Camera." Do this very loudly so that everyone can hear you. Then they will know that you are the one in charge.

2. Talk about movies that no one has heard of. If you don't know any, just make some up. No one has heard of them anyway, right? When making movie titles up, it often helps to make up titles in different languages. That way, no one will even understand what you are saying, so how can they prove you wrong?

3. Talk about other directors whose work you enjoy. As with the above tip, if you don't know of any directors, just make one up. This will show that you are the smartest person on the set, and thereby, the director.

4. Yell "Action" even louder than you yelled before. It is an unwritten rule in filmmaking that he who yells that loudest is the best director. Just ask James Cameron. Yelling also gets everyone's adrenaline pumping. Legendary director Samuel Fuller was known to fire a gun instead of yelling "action," but if I had a gun around, I'd be too tempted to blow my brains out instead.

5. When something goes wrong, sigh. Sigh a lot.

By using all of the valuable nuggets of information and wisdom I have imparted in the previous eight chapters, you have now completed principal photography, at least in principle. Unless your day job is running a school, in which case, you will have completed principal's principal photography, in principle.

DIRECT YOUR OWN DAMN MUSIC VIDEO

One of the easiest (and fun) ways to get into directing is to direct a music video. They are usually short (less than 5 minutes) and you don't have to spend weeks pondering what song will go perfectly with your artistic car chase — the music is chosen for you! Also, and this is huge, the band and/or record label will usually put up the cash. After all, having a well-directed and produced music video to show around can only benefit the career of the garage band next door. And let's face it, everybody knows at least one dude who is "working here at Chili's, but really in a band . . ." Many of those guys are perfectly willing to put up a couple hundred (or thousand) dollars to jumpstart their career and make it big. If they don't spend the money on a music video, they'll just spend it on cocaine anyway, so you're really doing them a favor!

In my career, I've been asked to direct several music videos, usually by bands who are outside of the mainstream cookie-cutter world of VH1. I directed one such video for the Lunachicks for the song, "Say What You Mean". The version that we shot and edited was great and the band loved it. Their record label, Go-Kart Records, however, asked for a second version. Our original footage was re-edited and that second version eventually ended up on MTV. The good news is that my name was still on it. The bad news is that I'm pretty sure my name was spelled incorrectly. That shoot was also the last time I did a whippit.* so the version I put together might have been a little out there.

We also shot a video for the song "Seeing Red" by Entombed. I had just gotten off the plane in Stockholm and I have to admit I was pretty sleep deprived. We immediately went to a theater and filmed a bunch of lesbians making out in the audience. The video turned out way cool, but the material was a little too spicy at the time to get in to the mainstream. Now, you could probably re-edit that footage, set it to a Miley Cyrus song and play it in heavy rotation on the Disney Channel.

Most recently, I flew to Minneapolis to direct a video for the band Faggot. The concept of the video was the band playing deep inside the

---

* EDITOR'S NOTE: I'm not sure that you mean by "did a whippit," Lloyd. The last time I checked, the correct spelling is "whippet" and it is a small dog, closely resembling a greyhound . . .

lead singer's ass. Before I arrived, diligent crew members had constructed a large anus for the set. For hours, dozens of beautiful women and dirty old bearded men writhed in fake blood and excrement. It was like being back in college!

What really sets these videos apart from most of the drivel you see on MTV (or MTV6 — whatever channel is actually playing music videos these days) is that they were all shot on film. The experience was similar to making a complete movie, but in miniature. Also, it isn't necessary to be so concerned about plot, and dialogue is almost non-existent, so that certainly helped me out! Shooting on film is not only great experience for you, but it helps the video really stand out.

If shooting the entire video on film causes some financial strain, try doing what we did for a Municipal Waste video. We shot the band performance on video and then intercut that with some classic Troma footage, which had, of course, originally been shot on film. Of course, you may not have 40 years of films from which to cull your footage. In that case, invest in a good HD camera and start rocking!

FIGURE 8.7 *Lloyd Kaufman, surrounded by Faggots and Faggot supporters. And by Faggots, we of course mean members of the band Faggot.*

Chapter nine

Postproduction, or Taking a Cue from Dedicated Hookers and Finishing Your Movie Off Right

The most important thing that you as a director should remember when principal photography wraps is that YOU'RE NOT DONE! A movie doesn't transform from a box of DV tapes sitting in your living room (or miles of 35 mm film sitting in your Tromaville office) into a real movie until it reaches postproduction — the editing, sound mixing, etc. When a gyno lovingly nurtures a fetus for nine months, feeding it from her own body through a bloody little tube, she doesn't just pop the kid out and consider her job finished,[1] assuming that someone else will care for it and make sure it comes

---

[1] Unless that gyno's name is Juno and she's a mouthpiece for an aging stripper.

out all right.[2] You need to treat your film like a fussy infant.** You've brought it through conception (the canoodling), preproduction (the morning sickness), and principal photography (the incredibly painful vagina-ripping birth). Now it's time to finish this baby up and send it off to college so that when you're old and unable to feed yourself, it might take care of you. Or put you away in an old-folks home.

FIGURE 9.1 *Lloyd Kaufman, circa 1966, surprised to learn that movie cameras don't actually suck out the soul of the person being filmed.*

---

[2] Or she's an Alaskan governor running for vice president. Or Katie Couric.*

    * EDITOR'S NOTE: Please stop, Lloyd. Both of these fine non-males are wonderful mothers and terrific role models.

** DISGRUNTLED FOOTNOTE GUY SAYS: I actually liked *Juno*. It was a very heartwarming story. You know, I'm starting to realize that most of these footnotes are pretty fucking stupid. I consider several of these an insult to my profession.

A LATE NIGHT PHONE MESSAGE FROM KURLY IN THE MIDDLE OF WRITING THIS CHAPTER

"Lloyd, it's Kurly. I don't want to let you down, but I am having some intense physical, emotional, financial, and mental problems. It would probably be best if you got someone else to finish the book. Sorry, Lloyd. . ."

MY FIRST PHONE CALL IMMEDIATELY AFTER RECEIVING THIS MESSAGE

"Sara, it's Lloyd. Kurly just quit. You know what that means . . ."

"I'll start working on the next chapter."

"Right. And then e-mail Kurly and get his fucking notes. And we need to talk about editing this Eli Roth interview. Did that theater in Pittsburgh pay us yet? Oh, and I need two tickets to Yemen."

OOPS! I DID IT AGAIN . . . AND OTHER POP REFERENCES FROM 1998

As thorough as you might be during preproduction and principal photography, the reality is that some things will be missed. That scene that you'd hoped would make sense will be a jumbled mess. The epic explosion that you planned will be less than impressive. The shitty performance you thought you'd be able to fix in editing will prove unfixable. Sometimes everything will look great, but you'll realize that you could use a little more connective tissue to tie the story together. The point is that, very often, you will need to go back and do some reshooting. If you have set aside some money in your budget for this ahead of time, it shouldn't be a problem.[3] But that's just my suggestion. Maybe you'll be the first person in history to get everything right the first time. But I imagine that if you were that knowledgeable, you would be working for Rupert Murdoch and not reading this shitty book.

REASON FOR RESHOOTING #1 — MY LOVE FOR DEBBIE ROCHON

Debbie Rochon, scream queen and Troma legend, was originally going to play the role of "Pregnant Mother" in *Poultrygeist*. Debbie

---

[3] I believe that this is one of Woody Allen's cardinal rules of filmmaking, and ranks just after marrying one's daughter.

came up from Manhattan to Buffalo, learned her lines, rehearsed energetically, and then left without filming the scene. "Why?" you might ask. Like the explanation for so many other things in Tromaville, it's because I was being an asshole. Apparently Debbie and our young lead actress Kate Graham didn't get along. Now, Debbie had done about 10 films for us, from *Tromeo & Juliet* and *Terror Firmer* to *Citizen Toxie*, and if I'd been behaving like a friend to Debbie or even a very good director, I would have addressed the situation and diffused it before it came to a boiling point. However, I was behaving like neither a friend nor a good director, and was preoccupied with troublesome transforming chicken zombie generals and fountains of brown water that were supposed to resemble explosive diarrhea.[4] As it was, I couldn't have fired Kate without causing major problems with the film, but I could have at least arranged a nice cat fight in tapioca pudding or something similarly entertaining. Instead, Debbie returned to Manhattan and we found another Pregnant Mother.[5] While in the editing room several months later, I suddenly awoke from a fugue state and realized that Debbie wasn't in the final film. To repay Debbie for all of her hard work for Troma over the years kissing girls and hanging by a rope from the ceiling while playing a pregnant woman, we brought her over to Hell's Kitchen and filmed a short scene on the roof of Troma headquarters where she's hit in the head with a plastic cup of beer and then assaulted by Elske McCain's large bouncing breasts. I can only hope that scene made up for my bad behavior.[6]

WHAT I LEARNED FROM THIS: Pay attention to shit.

WHAT YOU SHOULD LEARN FROM THIS: Do whatever it takes to get Debbie Rochon in your movie. Also, pay attention to shit.

---

[4] Not a special effect, in fact, but some of my own explosive diarrhea due to some unfortunate eggplant parmesan.

[5] I chose the costume designer, Tessa Lew, who suffered plenty. See *Poultry in Motion*, the *Poultrygeist* behind-the-scenes edu-mentary for a few examples of just how she suffered, such as sitting in make-up, not being able to see, for 7 hours. She's actually quite lucky that no farmer came around and tried to drown her like a baby kitten.

[6] I hope it did, because a few short months later, Debbie came to a *Poultrygeist* press party on the Lower East Side and filmed the *Best of TromaDance Film Festival Volume 5* DVD intro with me, in which she allowed us to make fun of her brain tumor. Just another reason why we love Debbie Rochon!

REASON FOR RESHOOTING #2 — GETTING YOUNG BOYS IN BED

Several of the special effects in *Poultrygeist* went very, very wrong the first time around. One that worked perfectly, though, was the exploding American Chicken Bunker at the end of the film. Coincidentally, this was also the effect that involved the fewest number of crew members and was filmed after principal photography had wrapped. We knew ahead of time that there would be no need for 80 tired and hostile crew members to stand around for the explosion, so we deliberately scheduled it for postproduction. Gabe Friedman, Kiel Walker, and myself drove up to Rochester, New York, to bring the American Chicken Bunker model to the pyrotechnics guy who would be doing the explosion. While there, Gabe and Kiel shared a motel room with me, which was quite a step up from the floor of the church where they had been sleeping for the past two months.

> WHAT I LEARNED FROM THIS: Kiel sleeps with a beauty mask over his eyes. Also, he snores. A lot. I also learned that Gabe and Kiel enjoy sleeping in the same bed . . . or was that just my fantasy . . .?
> WHAT YOU SHOULD LEARN FROM THIS: Schedule your shoot wisely. Also, hire beautiful young boys like Gabe and Kiel, and then force them to accompany you on trips. Also, claim that you only have enough cash for one motel room.

CUTTING, PASTING, AND OTHER SKILLS I WOULD HAVE LEARNED IN PRESCHOOL IF MY MOTHER HADN'T RUINED MY LIFE BY KEEPING ME AT HOME UNTIL 10TH GRADE

I consider myself rather agnostic regarding technology, especially as it pertains to film editing. There are several options out there, and I'll leave it up to you to decide which one works best for you. At Troma, we edited with Avid for 10 years before recently switching to Final Cut Pro.[7] Back when we started Troma and edited on 35mm celluloid, editing was a group effort. You needed a supervising editor, one or two assistant editors, and several interns to log footage, reconstitute

---

[7] I've heard rumors that Apple is coming out with Final Cut Semi-Pro, specifically for Troma editors. All the tutorials will be written in simple sentences, and all examples will refer to Troma's two favorite types of "pros" — football players and hookers.

trims,[8] and take notes. We used machines called Moviolas, Steenbecks, KEMS, Rivas Splicers, and rewinds. That was how I learned to edit. Now, with all these technological advances, you can do your own editing right out of the camera. Unfortunately, what John McCain knows about the economy, I know about computerized editing. I never actually learned how to do it, so I do, in fact, still need an editor.

Even when you're not editing yourself, you, as director, should still be in total control of the editing process. The actual editor is a tool to be wielded. When young Gabe Friedman came to work at Troma in 1929, fresh out of NYU Film School,[9] our relationship was largely dictatorial. As in, I would tell him to edit something a certain way, he would tell me it was a bad idea and that I should go fuck myself, and then he would edit it the way I told him to. Over time, I came to respect Gabe's opinion and we essentially flipped positions.[10] As in, I would tell him to edit something a certain way, he would tell me it was a bad idea and that I should go fuck myself, and then I would agree to whatever he suggested. But this type of beautiful relationship takes years and years to develop. In the beginning, the editor should be subservient to you.

SELF-LOVE . . . RON JEREMY STYLE

When someone is acting as the writer, the director, and the producer of a film, often they are too in love with their own work. That's why a good director has to find a really good editor to say, "The film is four and a half hours long. I love you but that has to be cut out!" Directors who love their work so much that they don't want to cut have a big problem. You have to cut — to make the movie fast and jumping and good. That is what keeps the audience interested. Directors often make the mistake of taking over too much of the editing because they love their work so much that they won't leave anything out.

---

[8] Speaking of trims, one of our assistant editors during *Sgt. Kabukiman* got some hot monkey love one evening in the Troma editing booth at 3 a.m., at least, according to the security cameras. The trim young woman was another assistant editor, and the two have been married ever since. To protect their privacy, I can't tell you who they are, but their first names are Donny and Marie.*

   *EDITOR'S NOTE: Lloyd, put down that Popov bottle, goddamit.

[9] Where Eli Roth was actually his advisor. Ha!

[10] Gabe and I also briefly considered flipping positions from missionary to blooming lotus, but Gabe has the arm strength of a 62-year-old man, and I actually am a 62-year-old man, so it just didn't work out.

A QUICK SIDEBAR ABOUT CONTROL

Here I am talking about having total control in the editing room, but in a way, that's bullshit. During the editing of *Poultrygeist*, my wife Pat, as Executive Producer, insisted on censoring two scenes — the shit coming out of Joe Fleishaker from the toilet cam[11] perspective, and the dancing scene where my balls are hanging out of my thong. You may not have a wife who cares enough about your balls to keep them to herself, but you'll still be dealing with censorship all along the way. You might expect censorship from the MPAA Ratings Board, but expect it from YouTube, iTunes, and other sites such as these as well. Blood, guts, and carnage are okay, but let a tit fall out during a wardrobe malfunction and the FCC might fine you $250,000. Let's not even talk about what might happen if a penis makes an appearance. Because if we start talking about that, I might get a little distracted.

GETTING INTO FOCUS

When you have a rough cut of the film, it's time to start showing it to people! One of the best ways to find out if the current cut of the film works or not is to show it to a focus group. Actually, I would suggest showing it to several focus groups. Ideally, the group would be coming into the screening blind,[12] unaware of what type of film they were about to see. With Troma films, this is especially difficult. We are one of the few film companies with a recognizable brand, and while that helps us 97% of the time, it makes finding objective focus groups a little more challenging. You shouldn't have as tough a time, as long as you go outside of your circle of family and friends. We showed *Poultrygeist* to four test audiences, one of which was in an actual theater in Ohio where people paid to get in. And only half of them demanded their money back. In the free screenings, the percentage demanding their money back was closer to 25%, which is still great for Troma.

Before the test screening, you should prepare a very simple multiple choice questionnaire. Ask the audience to rate the film 1 to 10,

---

[11]This soon-to-be famous toilet cam perspective involved building a fake Joe Fleishaker ass and holding it up against a fake toilet seat to create the illusion of the camera actually being in the toilet as shit spilled from the ass. Putting a camera in a real shit-filled toilet would have been just stupid — at least that's what Michael Herz told me. This technological breakthrough in filmmaking is still a Troma secret, however, so don't tell George Lucas!

[12]This joke is too easy. Make it yourself.

ask them if there are any questionable points in the story, anything they don't understand, anything they especially like, and so on. In *Poultrygeist*, we were worried that people wouldn't know why the General Chicken monster was exploding. Several thought it was due to global warming. One person didn't even realize that the monster had exploded. Needless to say, we re-worked and even re-shot the scene. When you watch the finished film, after the explosion, Wendy remarks, "Well, that was anti-climactic." We left that improvised line in there because it summed up our whole ordeal with that particular twice-failed effect, and that line always gets a laugh.

It isn't enough to just pass out the questionnaire, though. I often sit in the audience during the focus screenings and try to gauge people's reactions. That was how I knew to take out Humus' song[13] in *Poultrygeist*. I had been unsure about the song all along, but it was clear in every screening that the audience completely shut down during that scene, and it took them 10–15 minutes to get back into the story. This probably wouldn't have been so obvious simply based on questionnaires.

FIGURE 9.2 *Lloyd Kaufman, finally filming his long awaited* Schindler's List *sequel,* Schindler & Ahmadinejad.

---

[13] The song, "S-U-I-C-I-D-E," is a contemporary reflection on the Muslim experience in America. Unfortunately, it had nothing to do with chickens or zombies.

Occasionally, though, you may need to go against the test audience. When we screened *Citizen Toxie*, every single audience shut down during the scene where a black man was dragged behind a truck. At one particular NYU screening, there was one guy in the audience who was laughing at everything — just laughing his head off hysterically at every joke. He stopped laughing, however, during that scene, and didn't laugh one more time during the rest of the film. Every bit of common sense, as well as Gabe Friedman and my wife Pat, told me to take that scene out, but I thought it was important to leave it in to make a point and memorialize the heinous Texan sport of dragging black guys behind pickup trucks until their limbs are sanded off by the cement road. Michael Herz was the only one who backed me up, and that's because he's a good guy. And I tell him so every day.

FIGURE 9.3 *The late Heath Ledger shares a jocular moment with Lloyd Kaufman on the set of* Poultrygeist.

After taking your rough cut and tweaking and pinching it as needed, what you are left with is you final cut. Now it's time to make it beautiful.

SOUND MIXING, AS OPPOSED TO UNSOUND MIXING

Keeping control in the editing room might seem like common sense, but there is an aspect of postproduction that is every bit as important, yet often forgotten by beginning filmmakers — *sound design*.

Sound design is essentially taking all the components of a scene — the dialogue, the musical score, the footsteps, the farts, the air conditioner hum, the growling penis monster, etc., and making a mix which is synced with the final cut of the film.

When we received the sound effects track back for *Poultrygeist*, I was severely disappointed, to put it mildly. It seemed that the young guys who had designed the effects track had seen nothing of Troma except Jane Jensen's "boinging" nipple in *Tromeo & Juliet*, and had assumed we wanted our film to essentially be a cartoon. Every five seconds there was a sophomoric jiggle sound or a cow bell or a fart noise. Now, no one loves cows, farts, and cow fart noises more than I do, but what these guys didn't realize is that we throw a cartoony sound effect in maybe once or twice per film, not in every scene. In this case, I felt it was important enough to assert myself[14] and start the sound effects track from (chicken) scratch. I called poor Bernie Hayden, the wonderful head of Sound Dimensions[15] who was about to retire, and suggested that perhaps we could give this another go. This time, Gabe Friedman and I went down to the sound studio ourselves and clucked like chickens[16] for an entire day to get the zombie chicken sound effects right.

You may be thinking to yourself at this point,

"Gee Lloyd, I'm making a pretty realistic movie, and I don't have any zombie chickens in my film. How hard can it be to get everyday noises on film?"

Let me answer your question with a question. . .

"Aren't you the same asshole who asked me a stupid question back in Chapter Six?"

---

[14] Actually, Gabe Friedman said he would decapitate me and shit down my neck if I didn't "assert" myself. Another example of that beautiful relationship I was telling you about.

[15] Sound Dimensions had previously mixed and provided sound design for *Tromeo & Juliet*, *Terror Firmer*, and *Citizen Toxie*.

[16] I don't mean this as some sort of euphemism for Gabe and I yelling at the sound guys. I literally mean that we clucked like zombie chickens into a microphone.*

*FOOTNOTE GUY SAYS: Chicken clucking really gets me hot. Can I have Gabe's number?

Let's take a crowd scene as an example. You may be tempted to create a sound loop or "wallah"[17] here. This will result in the most boring crowd scene ever put on film. It's just as important for a crowd to have its performance depicted in sound as any other character in the film. Each actor–person should have her own sound, just like every chicken zombie needs its own sound. The voice/sound of the General monster in *Poultrygeist* was a combination of 57* different sounds, including a donkey, an elephant, and a lion. It's this sound attention to sound detail that will set your film apart from the ones that suck. One final mistake that I continue to make (because I am so cheap) is not creating an M&E track during the final mix. M&E refers to a music and effects track. With this track, all English dialogue is removed so that the film can be dubbed into different languages.** Unfortunately, this costs extra money. Don't be as cheap as I am and try to save money here. An M&E track is the an important thing to have.

NOT AS RACIST AS IT SOUNDS . . . REALLY

In the same way that you carefully watched over the shoulder of your sound designers, it is also vital to spend some time in the lab with the person working on the film's color correction. This person, known as a Timer, is the one to take each shot and decide on the color. She will make sure that the sky is the same color of blue in each frame and that people don't change from pasty white to beach volleyball player tan during a single conversation. In these crazy modern times, many labs will let computers do the color correction. I'm not a huge fan of this, as computers generally lack the distinguishing palate of an artist. If your color correction is handled by a computer, just

---

[17] The sound that a depressed director will make just after throwing himself off the Queensboro Bridge.

* EDITOR'S NOTE: This is not one of Lloyd's humorous exaggerations. I checked it out and it really was 57 different sounds.

    LLOYD'S RESPONSE: Yep, and it will soon debut as a Heinz 57 Relish!

    EDITOR'S RESPONSE: Okay, I'm pretty sure that's not true. But I think this book is causing me to lose my (chicken) shit detector.

    LLOYD'S RESPONSE: Good one!

** EDITOR'S NOTE: Lloyd's movies dubbed into another language?? Ha! That'll be the day. . . . He should save his money and forget the M&E. I imagine Lloyd has more use for M&Ms!

be sure to watch over that computer's shoulder just like you, as the anal retentive bastard that you are, would watch over a human being.

THE ANSWER!

Once the color and sound have been properly adjusted, the first print — the first 35 mm print of your fabulous film — is known as an answer print. That's because it is the answer to all your problems. And the beginning of a whole set of new ones.

BUT WHAT ABOUT THE OTHER 99% WHO AREN'T SHOOTING ON 35 MM?

If you aren't shooting on film, that doesn't mean you're off the hook. You have an even better chance to improve your own damn movie at the final stage of video color correcting.

A CONVERSATION OVER THE INTERCOM AT THE TROMA BUILDING

(BEEP)

LLOYD: Sara! What do you call the final stage of video?

SARA: Hang on a second, Lloyd. I'm on the other line with a guy who wants to book a movie.

LLOYD: Well hang up the fucking phone! I need to know what the final stage of digital video is.

SARA: I don't know what you're talking about.

LLOYD: Video! What do you call it?

SARA: I can ask Travis.[18] Hang on.

LLOYD: Yes, Travis will know. Find out.

SARA: Wait, Travis is standing right here. I'll ask him.

LLOYD: Don't ask him now. I have other things to do. Just find out.

SARA: But he's right here and I don't understand what you mean.

(CLICK)

(BEEP)

SARA: Travis. What do you call the final stage of video?

TRAVIS: What?

SARA: I don't know. Maybe the final master? Can you ask Lloyd what he means. I don't know why he wouldn't just let me ask you. I swear,

---

[18] Troma's current editor and resident terminology expert.

this place is going to kill me. One day he's going to ask me something and I'm just going to blow my fucking brains out.

TRAVIS: You sound like Lloyd.

(CLICK)

(TEN MINUTES LATER)

(BEEP)

TRAVIS: Hey.

SARA: Hey.

TRAVIS: The master is called a Digi-Beta. As in, the digital master is connected to the word beta.

SARA: Great.

TRAVIS: You know, Lloyd just wanted to know so he could make a master-beta joke.

SARA: I know.

(CLICK)

During the telecine[19] stage, you can supervise the color that will be on your final digital master, and you can also have the gyno doing the telecine re-frame scenes. For example, in *Poultrygeist*, we made a rather big boo-boo. There is a close-up of Wendy, played by the adorable Kate Graham, with a "Store Closed" sign in the frame. The sign should have read "Store Open" so I asked the telecine dude to zoom in on Wendy and frame out the sign. You can also do this on film, but it is insanely expensive and must be done by an optical effects house. You also lose a generation of film, which means that the quality of that particular shot will suffer and not look as good as the rest of the scene. I consider this a distraction worse than the continuity problem. Because of this difference between fixing the problem on film and fixing it digitally, the DVDs of my fowl movement do not have this error because the "Store Closed" sign has disappeared. However, the 35 mm prints shown in cinemas do have this glaring error.*

---

[19] The process of allowing footage originally shot on film to be viewed on standard video.

* A NOTE FROM SARA: *Poultrygeist* has been shown in about 300 cinemas, universities, and festivals, and not once has anyone commented on this so-called continuity error. Kind of makes a person wonder if anyone is really paying attention . . .

LLOYD'S RESPONSE: It probably has something to do with a Twizzler and concession stand food-induced fugue state of mind. How else would you explain someone sitting through *Speed Racer*?

FIGURE 9.4 *This is one of the few pictures from* Poultrygeist *where Lloyd Kaufman's balls aren't hanging out of his costume, and consequently, one of the few that we're allowed to show you.*

WHEN IT'S ALL SAID AND DONE . . .

Your film is finished. Pat yourself on the back, sit back, kick your feet up, and wait for the depression to set in. You've devoted months, maybe years to getting your film finished, and now what? It ain't called postpartum depression for nothing! As empty as you might feel, don't despair! You've come to the end of one road, and it's time to embark on another journey — distribution.

Chapter ten

If You Want It Done Right, You've Got to Do It Yourself, or Pay Someone a lot of Money

One of the most interesting pieces of feedback that I've ever received following a screening of one of my films occurred just a few months ago at a *Poultrygeist* screening at the Avignon Film Festival. I'd done a short introduction to the movie, and then stepped outside to bum a cigarette off an adoring fan. (If your last name is Kaufman and you are my wife or one of my daughters, then I had simply stepped outside to get a breath of fresh air. Hear that, Charlotte?) As I was taking in one particularly satisfying drag of fresh air, I was approached by an audience member who had somehow torn herself away from the chicken carnage inside.

"That is an interesting artistic choice, Monsieur Kaufman. To cut the heads off like that."

"Oh, yes, thank you. Merci! Chevrolet coup de ville!"

I smiled, and then began to think about the statement. The zombie massacre scene in *Poultrygeist* had peoples' faces being ripped off and then eaten like chicken skin. A guy's face was eaten by chicken nuggets. Someone else's face was deep fried. But had I really allowed so banal an effect as someone's head simply being cut off? And she had said heads, as in plural.

"*Excusez-moi*. Which heads, exactly, do you mean?"

The young woman looked at me and cocked her head to the side. She put her hand up just above her nose.

"The heads being cut off. Right here."

Confused, and more than slightly concerned, I went back into the dark theater. On the screen, I saw the faces of Jason Yachanin and Kate Graham. Scratch that . . . I saw their faces from the nose down. The projectionist had somehow framed the film incorrectly or angled the projector just badly enough to almost be humorous. Almost. This soon became a mini-nightmare as we discovered that "le projectionist" had taken a powder and locked the projection booth. Eventually, after a loud *sacre bleu*! and cinema workers running around like chickens with their heads cuts off, "le projectionist" showed up, puzzled about what all the commotion was about. Three years of making *Poultrygeist* only to have its French premiere fowled by bad projection was not as serious a matter to him as the *jambon et fromage baguette* he was searching for.[1] I made him start the film again from the beginning. Not everyone in the audience was appreciative of this. In the middle of all of it, though, all I could think was how oddly that woman must think of me to assume that I had intentionally filmed everyone from the nose down.

CONGRATULATIONS . . . I'M SORRY (AND OTHER POP CULTURE REFERENCES FROM 1996)

I often get into quite a funk after a film is completed. And considering that I've already admitted that I'm in a funk during much of preproduction and production, it might seem like I spend much of my film-making life in a funk. But the truth is, there is nothing much more exciting than watching an audience watch your film — for the first time or the 4,367th time. And even though it becomes increasingly more difficult to get a mainstream publication to pay attention to an

---

[1] *Direct Your Own Damn Movie* Lesson #878: If it is an important screening, you, as director, should stay in the theater to make sure the projectionist doesn't fuck it up.

independent film, I have had few better days in my life than the day I woke up to *Poultrygeist's* rave review in *Entertainment Weekly*.[2] You made your film so that people could see it, right? So the film is finished and since then you've spent a good three months in your basement crying about the lack of direction in your life. What now?

SNAP OUT OF IT! Get out there and whore for your art. Do everything you, as director, can possibly do to get the media to take note of your film.

FIGURE 10.1 *Lloyd Kaufman accepts the NAMBLA Lifetime Achievement Award, 1952.*

PUTTING THE "I" IN FESTIVAL

Film Festivals are a great way to get your film out there for people to see. You've heard of the biggies like Cannes and Sundance. But the sad truth is that, unless your film stars Dakota Fanning or Steve Carell and costs upwards of $12 million, the chances of getting your

---

[2] The day that each of my daughters was born ranks up there too, but I've got to admit that the *Entertainment Weekly* review was pretty nice. Owen Gleiberman gave our fowl movie a B+, and in the same issue, gave *Indian Jones: Curse of the Past-its-Prime Movie Franchise* only a B−!

film shown at Sundance are pretty slim. Like, Mary Kate Olsen slim. Back in 1883, two young filmmakers by the name of Trey Parker and Matt Stone submitted their film *Cannibal! The Musical* to the Sundance Film Festival and paid a hefty submission fee for the privilege. Not only did their film, which went on to become a Troma classic, NOT get into the festival, but they received not so much as a letter, phone call, e-mail, or courier pigeon with a note saying "Fuck You!" tied to its foot. Out of this slight to Trey and Matt, the TromaDance Film Festival was born. Each year Troma holds its own festival in Park City, Utah, at the same time as Sundance. We charge no admission fee for filmmakers to enter their movies, nor do we charge admission to any of the screenings. As such, TromaDance has absolutely no revenue. So take that, Sundance!

FIGURE 10.2 *Lloyd Kaufman and Trey Parker, on their yearly pilgrimage to Del Taco.*

There are several film festivals going on all over the world at any one time. Do some creative Google-ing and start sending your film out.

WHEN IT'S OKAY TO SELL OUT

When your film does begin to show publicly, which I'm sure it will if you've followed the sage wisdom in this book so far, you should be sure that those involved in the distribution process show as much concern for your film as you have. This includes everyone from the projectionist in the theater to the Troma acquisitions man–boy to the angry exec at Fox Searchlight who pays you a big advance for your distribution rights. Stanley Kubrick actually used to sit in the projection booth to be sure that the fat slob managing[4] 13 screens didn't play reel #3 before reel #1 or project "à la Avignon." We at Troma get calls every day from filmmakers whose films we acquired two years ago, wondering when the film will actually be released on DVD. We don't actually answer these calls, but that doesn't mean that I don't encourage you to make similar calls if someone acquires your film. Never be afraid to get in there and make yourself heard. When your film is finally released, talk to the media. Reviewers don't want to hear from a Public Relations guy. If they listen to any-one, it will be you. You are a D-I-R-E-C-T-O-R!

A NOTE FROM SARA, LLOYD'S (UP UNTIL NOW) LOYAL ASSISTANT

Wait Lloyd, what's going on? You're talking about distribution now? Distribution isn't a director's job, is it? I thought this book was supposed to be about directing. Did I miss that part?

Seriously, Lloyd, so far you've talked about how to be a script supervisor, how to be an editor, how to do PR, and how to blow up a fucking chicken monster, which I swear, if I have to hear about one more time I'm just going to lose it. Have I ever reminded you that I moved to New York specifically to work for you? And not just New York, but to Queens! I'm starting to think that this is all just bullshit. *Poultrygeist* was shot in, what, 2005? It's 2008 now. That's three fucking years of you NOT directing movies. I expected to be on a movie set by now, sleeping on the floor and eating cheese sandwiches and learning how to defecate in a paper bag. That's what your other books were about. Instead, for the last six months you've been wandering around the office muttering something about "looking for an ensemble piece." Is there some new project in the works that I don't know about? I kind of doubt it, seeing as I'm the one who answers your phone and checks your e-mails while you're running around France "promoting" *Poultrygeist*. Well, congratulations. *Poultrygeist* opened well and still got kicked out of the theater so *Indiana Jones Part IV*

---

[4] And by manage, I mean eat a bologna sandwich in the general vicinity of the projector while chatting on the phone with his pot dealer and watching TV.

could open on 72,000 screens in New York alone. Oh yeah, we got some decent reviews. And then there was that shitty review in *The Washington Post* where the guy didn't even watch the movie and still hated it. God, sometimes I come to work and the phone doesn't even ring. Some days I get more comments on my Facebook than e-mails relating to Troma business. And then I finally do find us a deal (with FRANCE!) and it falls through. Why? Because there's no M&E track,

FIGURE 10.3 *Thank God* Poultrygeist *was kicked out of the theater to make room for* Indiana Jones *so Lloyd Kaufman didn't feel obligated to spend any more money on ads like this one!*

which you promised you would make this time. When are you going to start following your own advice?

Even here, in this book, I don't understand you. Here is this opportunity to write a book on directing and secure yourself some kind of legacy in the film world, and what do you do? You spend 200 pages talking about fucking chickens. . . . Yeah, that's right . . . 200 pages! Not 322 pages like your contract said. Nice work.

Where is the directing, Lloyd? Where's all the advice on seeing through the lens with a poet's eye, or some shit like that! Seriously, does James Gunn need an assistant? I bet if he wrote a book about directing, it would actually be about directing. That guy left Troma and two seconds later was writing *Scooby Doo*. And here I am, working on writing that introduction to your lesson on fart noises. And to top it all off, I just found out that people who intern on reality shows make twice as much money as I do, and THEY ARE ON STRIKE FOR MORE MONEY! I think you should find someone else to work on this book. I really need to reevaluate my life . . .

In fact, you know what? I quit.

A CONVERSATION WITH ELINOR, MY EDITRIX

I am in my office. It's late. Michael is gone. The Troma Team is gone. The neighbors are quiet. Both of my cowriters have abandoned this book. It's just me and my friend Popov. The phone rings.

"Hello Lloyd? It's Elinor."

"Oh, Elinor. What a surprise! How are you? Good?"

I take a long, burning sip from the vodka bottle.

"Say, Elinor, did you get the last chapter of the book? I think it's pretty good."

"It's fine Lloyd. I just —"

"Yep, I really think it's done Elinor. I think we've covered it all."

"About that, Lloyd. We're just a little confused here. You say this is the last chapter?"

"Yep, that's it. All finished! That's all she wrote. I mean, metaphorically. I mean, that's it."

(Insert pregnant pause here . . .)

"Well, Lloyd, I'm not sure how to say this, but let me be blunt. Is this book about directing? I mean, if you want to call the book something else, maybe we could find another title, but I'm not sure that directing is really the focus here . . ."

(I stand up here. I'm not sure why, since Elinor is on the phone and can't see me. Maybe I just feel more authoritative standing up.)

"Did my assistant Sara ask you to say that?"

"What? Lloyd, I don't even know your assistant. Maybe you should sit down."

(I sit down here. Again, I'm not sure why. I also don't know how she knew I was standing in the first place).

"Listen, Elinor. There's a lot of stuff in this book. I know that. But it's all directing. It is! A director doesn't just stand in front of the camera and say "action." A director needs to know the script. He needs to know casting. He needs to know how to get his movie seen. He needs to know how to make fucking zombie chicken noises!"

"Well, that's the other problem Lloyd. There's a lot of stuff here, but it's only 176 pages.

"Yep."

"Your contract stated 322 pages. We're not really sure what to do with all of this, Lloyd."

"Elinor, you don't know what it's been like here. This has been tough. I've been hallucinating the Toxic Avenger and everyone is quitting on me and there was this bookshelf, Elinor . . . this fucking bookshelf. . ."

"Okay, calm down. Calm down a little."

"And I keep getting e-mails from someone working on the foot-notes. What does he want from me?"

"Calm down, Lloyd. Are you calming down?"

"Yes, Elinor." I take another swig from the bottle.

"Maybe you could just do one more chapter just about directing for us. Maybe something artistic, like looking through the lens with a poet's eye, or something like that."

"Seriously, Elinor, did my assistant call you? Because she's not here anymore, so —"

"Lloyd, can you have that chapter to me by tomorrow?"

(Insert another pregnant pause here . . .)

"Sure Elinor."*

---

* LONELY FOOTNOTE GUY SAYS: I'm still with you Lloyd. Wanna come over?

Chapter eleven

A Chapter Just About Directing

HOW TO DIRECT A MOVIE

1. Point a camera at something.
2. Turn the camera on.
3. Make a movie.
4. Don't kill anyone.

FIGURE 11.1

THE END*

*A NOTE FROM YOUR FRIENDLY FOOTNOTE GUY: Lloyd, I just want to say that I feel like we've been through a lot together on this book. There have been a lot of ups and downs, but I feel they have only brought us closer. I don't know if I ever told you this, but back when I was studying fine print in school, I roomed with a guy named Leon, who ended up doing the end credits for you on *Tromeo & Juliet*. We keep in touch, and just the other day we were talking about what an inspiration you've been to both of us. In fact, we decided to take the advice herein and write our own book. We are going to call it *Write Your Own Damn Footnote!* We want to dedicate the book to you, Lloyd. I love you.

Focal Press
An imprint of Elsevier Science
www.focalpress.com

October 9, 2008

Dear Lloyd,

I'm not sure if you have been receiving all of my emails, as many editorial notes within those emails have not been addressed. These range from relatively minor concerns such as use of offensive and/or inappropriate language, to much larger concerns including, but not limited to, numerous libel issues and the overall direction of the book.

I hope you know that we love you over here at Focal Press, but I have been advised by our legal team to inform you that failure to meet the agreed upon length of 322 pages will result in nullification of contract.

Essentially, you will not be paid.

Please let us know what you intend to do to rectify this unfortunate situation.

Best regards,

Elinor

----------------------------Original Message--------------------------
From: Lloyd Kaufman <lloyd@troma.com >
Sent: October 10, 2008 8:44PM
To: Elinor <elinor@repress.com >
Subject: RE: Okay, okay

Dear Elinor,

Okay, I'm starting to get that you want some more pages. Here are a few last minute but important and practical directing tips, in case you missed the rest of the book.

xoxo
Angelina Jolie's left twin

----------------------------End Message----------------------------

SEVEN QUICK DIRECTING TIPS FOR THE ROAD

Sean McCoy

Last Minute but Important and Practical Directing Tip #1

Use mirrors. Shoot into them. You can get hard-to-reach shots and it makes for good eye movement (mise-en-scène) around your frame. Where a Hollywood film might buy a ceiling fan, build a contraption to suspend it four feet down from the ceiling, and shoot their shot down through the spinning blades, you can use duct tape (or even have someone hold) a mirror to the ceiling and shoot into that to get the exact same shot for almost no money. In tight spaces such as cars you can shoot into mirrors or use the three already provided for fun angles and with a little forethought and a steady hand, you won't even have to hang out a window to shoot your cast. Half of the time mirrors are already incorporated into your settings or shooting locations and can be played with in too many interesting ways to pass them up. If they're not in your setting, but they could be, then put them in and use them!

Last Minute but Important and Practical Directing Tip #2

Never turn your camera on its side or upside down during a shot. It's unprofessional, and worse than that, it looks completely awful. Unless you have rigged an extremely smooth and controlled tracking device for its motion, people will notice every little jerk and shake. It will make people think more of a home movie rather than any kind of art. It's distracting and can be somewhat nauseating, so unless you're Gaspar Noé, or you're trying to remake *The Blair Witch Project,* you should concentrate more on content and framing than exaggerated camera motions.

Last Minute but Important and Practical Directing Tip #3

If you shoot in color and you intend your end product to be in color, then use color. It can be difficult, even with digital video, to pull the kinds of colors you want from a scene, and most of the time, it's really not worth the cash it takes to have complete color palette for each set you shoot on. Instead, spend $20 at a hardware store and get a few primary colored lights (red, blue and yellow). If a scene is violent or tense, aim a red light at the ceiling to give everything in the room a slight tint. Keep in mind that no matter what you see through your camera at the time, if you are using neon lights on your set, everything will come out with a slight green tint. These colors will affect your audience's feelings in a subconscious way and will add some nice depth to your shots. Using the colors in the opposite way is also interesting — a calm blue for a horribly tragic or violent scene can make your audience as uncomfortable as nails on a chalkboard, if that's what you're going for.

Last Minute but Important and Practical Directing Tip #4

Need music? Check out Myspace or other social networking sites. Just spend an hour or two searching out smaller, unknown bands by genre on Myspace. Many of those bands will let you use their music for free as long as you credit them and send them a copy of what you shoot. You will have made good contacts for future projects and people who may even help in getting your film shown wherever they live, since they had a part in it!

Last Minute but Important and Practical Directing Tip #5

Find a public place to show your film. Bars and coffee houses are great places, and if you're cool with them, they will likely charge you little or nothing. Invite your family and friends, and then track down one of those little digital projectors that can be hooked up to VCR and DVD players — sometimes local libraries lend them out. Just make sure you know how to use the thing before the showing!

Next, find every newspaper, TV news station, free paper and every 'zine address within forty miles of where you're showing your film. Write extremely professional and personalized promotional letters to any names you can round up from each media source. If you suck at writing, have someone else do it. Also, it's okay to lie in these letters, as long as you can be very convincing. If you think that you can make the reader believe that Bill Clinton is coming to your show, then do it. If you can convince them that MADD is protesting outside your showing because of an underage drunk driving scene in your film, then do it. Or heck, why not set up your own protest and call the papers yourself to scream about it. If there actually is an underage drunk driving scene in your film, then call MADD and complain about it. Get them to actually protest! Spike Lee did things like that all the time to promote his films. Just be careful — learn the law so you aren't breaking it. You don't need trouble, I don't need to get sued, and I'm sure Lloyd just doesn't want the hassle.

The point is, publicity is publicity, so go get some! Tricks and sneakiness are definitely allowed; just don't do anything stupid or dangerous. Or maybe just dangerous. If you're feeling immoral about all this manipulation, just think about it this way . . . a TV news station's ratings go up (and they get more money) when crazy events happen, because crazy stuff makes people watch more news. So why not shock them with your own devious, yet playful, madness. Jive 'em with something interesting! Unless your movie is a drama, in which case, you should probably try to arrange some kind of silent vigil with a lot of candles or something.

Last Minute but Important and Practical Directing Tip #6
Infiltrate the media. If there is a position open at a local paper, even if it's a custodial position, take it. Custodian work can actually be kind of cool, if you go in with the right attitude! But more to the point, you can learn the ropes by listening in on reporters. Make friends with them, even if you hate their guts. Just try to think like they do for a little while, no matter how raped your thoughts feel afterward. Besides, as my pal Gay Frank says, it's just your thoughts, not your ass. I still don't understand what that means, especially coming from him, but there it is.

But it's all for your movie! Start a buzz, but don't mention yourself. About a week before your premiere, mention to one of your new reporter friends that you and tons of your (real) friends are going to this movie showing. Let them know that you usually hate that kind of B-movie junk, but everyone and their mother has been talking about this thing for weeks, and if nothing else, you could all get wasted and cause a riot. In fact, that part might actually be true . . . Just keep at it. Mention the screening at least 4 out of 5 days that you talk to the reporters, but just make sure to be clever and nonchalant about it.

Last Minute but Important and Practical Directing Tip #7
Get a permit. Or don't get a permit. Or just read the following scenario and then decide . . .

The kid lay in the middle of the street, his brains blown out from the double yellow lines all the way to the curb. It was about two o'clock in the morning and he looked uncomfortable laying there, but he must have known that any movement would dislodge the jelly and foam-covered plastic head which had taken almost an hour to set up. The kid was so dedicated that he continued to lay there even after four police cruisers pulled up. I was on the roof of someone's apartment with one camera, Gay Frank was on the opposite roof shining lights on it all, and an actress was sitting next to the headless actor, waiting for her cue.

"What the hell are you doing?" shouted one of the cops to the terrified actress. "And what the hell is that in the street?"

The girl was too freaked to talk, but a string of muffled explanations came from under the exploded head on the ground.

"Hey, sorry," I said, out of breath from a run down the apartment building's fire escape. "We're just filming this movie —"

"Yeah, I can see what you're doing. Identification?"

"What?"

"Are you deaf? I said give me your ID!"

I jumped at the outburst and began fumbling in my back pocket trying to find my wallet.

"Chill out, okay. This is just a cheap indie film. We're not hurting anyone."

"You are inciting a panic."

I looked around. A few of the drunks in front of the bar across the street waved at me. A burly policewoman lumbered up to us.

"Goddamn, what the hell is that in the street?" she demanded, pointing at the splatter. I glanced over my shoulder. The actress looked about three seconds from tears, Gay Frank had gone MIA, and the kid (sans head) was still lying in the road, playing dead in a puddle of goo.

"We were going to clean it all up."

"Where's your filming permit?" the first cop asked.

I took a deep breath.

"Well, you see, first I went to City Hall and the guy at the front desk sent me to some lawyer upstairs, then the lawyer gave me the card of this judge, but neither of them knew where to get a permit so the judge told me to call the police chief."

Five policepersons had formed a semicircle around me and stood listening. Their radios chirped strange codes in a static monotone.

"So you talked to the chief?" said one young cop with a cocked eyebrow. One cop standing behind a cruiser raised a radio to his mouth and said, "No, it's just some kids with a camera. Looks like they're filming roadkill."

I brought my attention back to the young policeboy who had asked about talking to the chief.

"No, actually, I left him a voicemail and he never called me back."

As a moment of dopey looks passed between them, I was able to see Gay Frank smile from behind the camera I had been running on the roof — god love him! I rolled my eyes at him and one of the cops must have taken it personally.

"Okay, into the car."

"What?" I yelped, suddenly near panic.

As I scanned their faces for help, the whole semicircle of cops gave me the same collective and eerie cop-grin before one took my shoulder and led me over to a patrol car. The next forty-five minutes were filled with useless questions and plenty of scolding, followed with the complete scouring of all jelly and fake blood from the road with cups of water that were run down from my apartment nearby.

"Next time, get permission," a butch police-ogre said to me once I was free of the cruiser. "People see this kind of thing and get scared and they call us saying someone's been killed in the street."

"Uh-huh," I mumbled, thanking Hitchcock that I didn't get a ticket and already wondering how to ditch my original ending and instead somehow use whatever police footage Gay Frank had gotten from the rooftop.

The moral of this story? If you want a really cool and realistic police crime scene in your film for free, then hide a camera and blow someone's head up in the street.

So you decide. To get a permit or not to get a permit . . . that is the question. Whatever you decide, just don't sue me if you end up getting arrested. Is that long enough, Lloyd?

Afterword — My Happy Ending

I'll probably never be a household name.[1] And some nights, when it's just me and a Troma mug filled with coffee dregs and Vodka, alone in Long Island City, I tell myself that I'm okay with that. Then I listen to our neighbors in the apartment building next door scream about a stolen bicycle for 45 minutes, and I wonder why the hell we moved our offices to Long Island City. But *c'est la vie*, and a decent life it is. I've been able to direct movies for 40 years, and somehow stay off the streets while doing it.

If there is one piece of advice that you take away from this book, maybe it should be this:

Don't be me.

There was a guy who volunteered in medical research studies to raise money to make his first film. He ended up directing *Sin City*. We didn't get to see Jessica Alba naked, but at least we didn't have to see Mickey Rourke naked either. Be that guy.

There was a guy who shot a film in the convenience store where he worked. He essentially introduced Ben Affleck to the world.[2] Be that guy.

There was a guy who came to work at Troma as my assistant, and ended up writing *Scooby Doo*. Go figure. Be that guy.

All of these guys, and plenty more like them, actually did what you just read. They made their own damn movies. They aren't sitting alone in an office drinking Popov, scurrying to write the afterword to their book, just to meet some arbitrary minimum page requirement so that they can fulfill their literary contract and get paid.

---

[1] Actually, there is a Vodka called "Kaufman" in Moscow and a detergent called "Lloyd" in Oman. So I guess I am a household name.

[2] But I'm sure he's sorry.

FIGURE EM1 *Lloyd Kaufman beams after receiving the exclusive rights to the upcoming film* Danger Woman Part VI. *However, we, as responsible editors, can't tell you what he did to get those rights.*

But on nights like tonight, when I get a little down, I sometimes open up my 1993 laptop and navigate over to Myspace.

And I find out that my former assistant has changed my password.

And so I call her cell phone, trying to get the new password.

And then I have a long conversation with her boyfriend about why she refuses to come to the phone.

But once I do finally get the new password, I check my messages and find things like this . . .

Subject: Oh man, you're the man!

Lloyd! I just wanted to tell you what a fucking inspiration you have been to me. I fucking love you! Keep fighting!!

Peace out,
A.J. aka Superfly

Or this ...

Subject: Uncle Lloydie

Your movies have made me a better person. I want to be Tromette of the Month!

xoxo
Chrissy

Or this …

Subject: Toxie for President!!

Poultrygeist has reinstated my faith in, not only in your writing and acting ability, but also in the evolution of Horror-cheese in general.

Basically, I like seeing ANYTHING with Lloyd on the business end of a camera. The tradition of Troma will live on forever!

All hail Kaufman!
jojo

I didn't set out 40 years ago to be the president of the longest-running independent film company in the world. Honestly, Michael Herz and I just wanted to make movies. Back in those days, if someone had given us 2 million dollars and told us to remake *Gone With the Wind*, we might have done it. Believe it or not, I didn't want to NOT make money and NOT win Oscars. It just worked out that way. But I get to do something that Brett Ratner doesn't get to do. I get to read stuff like this. . .

Subject: Hey I was the guy from Chattanooga with the clove cigarette . . .

You were asking me about why I liked them but I think you should have been able to tell cause they were awesome. Also I think you were the most awesome person I met at DragonCon this year, its something I was dreaming about since I was 7 (ok back then it was meeting Toxie but still . . .) and I would willingly work for no pay on any project you may do, and it's not just an empty promise cause I have worked with no pay on a lot of indie movies around here as an actor, a PA, a boom mike guy, a folly artist . . . you name it, and damn it I would sure as hell drive to NYC or NJ to work on a Troma film for free.

Your eternal fan,
Peter

I had met Peter, a beautiful young boy, at DragonCon in Atlanta, Georgia, the week before. He had wanted to have a beautiful and heartwarming relationship in the men's bathroom of the Hilton, but I declined his offer.[3] With a sad smile and a wave, he was off to a *Battlestar Galactica* panel and gone from my life forever. But his kind words live on.

And I wouldn't trade shit like that for all the Oscars in the world.

FIGURE EM2 *Some of the wonderful fans who make Lloyd Kaufman's life worthwhile. Unfortunately, the happy moment was ruined when, shortly after these pictures were taken, the man on the top ate the woman on the bottom.*

[3]He weighed 400 lbs, and I'm married.

Lloyd Kaufman's Filmography

Film & Television

JACQUES DAMBOISE: THE OTHER SIDE OF THE WORLD (2008)
Documentary
Producer

POULTRY IN MOTION: TRUTH IS STRANGER THAN CHICKEN (2008)
Feature-Length Documentary
Executive Producer

SPLENDOR AND WISDOM: REV. WILLIAM SLOAN COFFIN AND THE YALE CLASS OF 1968 (2007)
Documentary
Writer, Director, Producer

POULTRYGEIST: NIGHT OF THE CHICKEN DEAD (2007)
Feature Film
Director/Co-writer/Producer

DOGGIE TAILS (2003)
Children's Film
Producer

TALES FROM THE CRAPPER (2003)
2 Feature Films
Producer/Actor

ALL THE LOVE YOU CANNES (2002)
Feature-Length Documentary
Co-Director/Co-Writer/Producer

CITIZEN TOXIE: THE TOXIC AVENGER PART IV (2000)
Feature Film
Director/Co-Writer of the Screenplay/Producer

TERROR FIRMER (1999)
Feature Film
Director/Co-Writer of the Screenplay/Producer

THE ROWDY GIRLS (1999)
Feature Film
Producer

DECAMPITATED (1998)
Feature Film
Executive Producer

SUCKER: THE VAMPIRE (1998)
Feature Film
Executive Producer

TROMEO & JULIET (1997)
Feature Film
Director/Co-Writer of the Screenplay/Producer

TROMAVILLE CAFE (1995)
Television Series
Director/Writer/Producer

CLASS OF NUKE 'EM HIGH (1993)
TV Pilot Script for Fox-TV
Co-Writer

TROMA INFOMERCIAL (1993)
Co-Director/Co-Writer/Co-Producer

PUBLIC SERVICE ANNOUNCEMENT (1992)
Anti-Pollution Spot for National Dance Institute
Producer

SGT. KABUKIMAN N.Y.P.D. (1991)
Feature Film
Co-Director/Co-Writer of the Screenplay/Co-Producer

THE SNAIL MUST GO THROUGH (1991)
TOXIC CRUSADERS TV Series Episode
Co-Writer

STILL CRAZY AFTER ALL THESE SHEARS (1991)
TOXIC CRUSADERS TV Series Episode
Co-Writer

THE GOOD, THE BAD AND THE SUBHUMANOID: CLASS OF NUKE 'EM HIGH PART III (1991)
Feature Film
Co-Writer of the Screenplay/Co-Producer

CLASS OF NUKE 'EM HIGH PART II: SUBHUMANOID MELTDOWN (1990)
Feature Film
Co-Writer of the Screenplay/Co-Producer

THE TOXIC AVENGER PART III: THE LAST TEMPTATION OF TOXIE (1989)
Feature Film
Co-Director/Co-Writer of the Screenplay/Co-Producer

FORTRESS OF AMERIKKKA (1989)
Feature Film
Producer/Writer of Narration

THE TOXIC AVENGER PART II (1989)
Feature Film
Co-Director/Co-Writer of the Screenplay/Co-Producer

TROMA'S WAR (1988)
Feature Film
Co-Director/Co-Writer of the Screenplay/Co-Producer

JAKARTA (1988)
Feature Film
Co-Executive Producer

MONSTER IN THE CLOSET (1987)
Feature Film
Executive Producer

LUST FOR FREEDOM (1987)
Feature Film
Executive Producer/Writer of Narration

CLASS OF NUKE 'EM HIGH (1986)
Feature Film
Co-Director/Co-Producer

GIRLS SCHOOL SCREAMERS (1986)
Feature Film
Executive Producer

BLOOD HOOK (1986)
Feature Film
Executive Producer

THE TOXIC AVENGER (1985)
Feature Film
Co-Director/Co-Writer of the Screenplay/Co-Producer

WHEN NATURE CALLS (1985)
Feature Film
Associate Producer

SCREAMPLAY (1984)
Feature Film
Executive Producer

THE FIRST TURN-ON! (1983)
Feature Film
Co-Director/Co-Producer

STUCK ON YOU! (1981)
Feature Film
Co-Director/Co-Writer of the Screenplay/Co-Producer

MY DINNER WITH ANDRE (1981)
Feature Film
Production Manager

MOTHER'S DAY (1980)
Feature Film
Associate Producer

WAITRESS! (1980)
Feature Film
Co-Director/Producer

SQUEEZE PLAY! (1979)
Feature Film
Director/Producer

THE FINAL COUNTDOWN (1979)
Feature Film
Associate Producer

SATURDAY NIGHT FEVER (1977)
Feature Film
Location Manager

SLOW DANCING IN THE BIG CITY (1977)
Feature Film
Production Supervisor

ROCKY (1976)
Feature Film
Pre-Production Supervisor

SWEET SAVIOR (1973)
Feature Film
Production Manager

BIG GUS, WHAT'S THE FUSS? (1972)
Feature Film
Director/Producer

THE BATTLE OF LOVE'S RETURN (1971)
Feature Film
Director/Writer/Producer/Actor

SILENT NIGHT, BLOODY NIGHT (1971)
Feature Film
Associate Producer

SUGAR COOKIES (1971)
Feature Film
Writer/Executive Producer

ALLEN FUNT PRODUCTIONS (1970)
Production Assistant

CRY UNCLE! (1970)
Feature Film
Production Manager/Limited Partner

JOE (1970)
Feature Film
Production Assistant

THE GIRL WHO RETURNED (1969)
Feature Film
Director/Writer/Producer

RAPPACCINI (1969)
Feature Film
Producer

Focal Press
An imprint of Elsevier Science
www.focalpress.com

October 13, 2008

Dear Lloyd,

I give up. 209 pages is enough.

Please stop writing.

Please.

Stop.

Best,

Elinor

Index

Page numbers followed by n indicate footnotes.

Printed in the United States
by LSC Taylor Publisher Services

Printed in the United States
by Baker & Taylor Publisher Services